Before COVID-19 swep
on earth to suspend i
of Americans were a
in a building. After returning to services, less th
Americans are attending. But while in-person attendance has declined, online viewership has exploded. It's time for the Church to go where the other 92% of people are because God's heart is after them, too. This book is a must-read for evangelism in every dimension.

—**NONA JONES**, bestselling author of *From Social Media to Social Ministry*, tech executive and pastor

Jason Moore has given us a gift in this book. *Both/And* is a welcome roadmap through the new, complex and sometimes frightening world of maximizing engagement in both our in-person and online worship experiences, without compromising either one. The ability to record and stream our services is now commonplace. But doing it well? That's not so common. That's where Jason comes in, with multiple options for creating a better worship experience for everyone. Doing hybrid worship is no longer a matter of access, money or equipment. Now it's about how well you use what you have. Churches of all sizes can gain a lot from the practical wisdom and experience Jason Moore writes about in *Both/And*.

—**KARL VATERS**, author, teaching pastor of Cornerstone Christian Fellowship, and resource provider for *Helping Small Churches Thrive* at KarlVaters.com

Jason Moore is a time-tested pioneer in understanding the necessity of creating new wineskins to hold new wine. I had the privilege of working with Jason in developing multisensory models of worship in the 1990's. Jason continues to move forward into God's next. This might be the most important read in 2022!

—**MIKE SLAUGHTER**, Passionate Churches LLC, Founder & Chief Strategist

Jason Moore has been a Godsend to thousands of churches the last two years as significant pivots were required in local church ministry. This is Jason's most timely and urgently needed book to date. As a ministry consultant with congregations in America and Europe, I can assure you that Both/And will be required reading for every church I work with in the days ahead. I have never said that before about any book. But I'm saying it now. Thanks, Jason!

—**PAUL NIXON**, CEO of Epicenter Group and co-author, *Launching a New Worship Community*

We all need someone in our corner. Jason Moore is a leader that can help you build momentum and design an effective strategy to win at both in-person and online church experiences. Churches and leaders across the country have benefited from his valuable experience as a practitioner and you can too. This is a book you need to read!

— **DR. JASON YOUNG**, author, keynote speaker, & executive coach at jasonyounglive.com

Jason's passionate heart and calling to equip churches is once again revealed through this incredibly timely book. Both/And Hybrid Worship is now a fixture in our present church ecology and this resource will help you and your church figure out how to navigate it. True to its name, it covers BOTH the practical AND the theological aspects of what hybrid worship and ministry might look like in your church context. You will easily find yourself represented somewhere in the book through a story, a process, or a reason to pursue hybrid worship. That's because the book firmly roots everything in RELATIONSHIPS - with God and with each other - regardless of if they are happening in-person or online. It's not either/or, it's BOTH/AND.

—**REV. ROB HUTCHINSON**, Director of Church Development, Western NC Conference of the UMC

No matter the size of your church, as a church leader you are sure to find multiple, timeless gems in Jason's strategies, checklists, and practical considerations to keep your church engaged in both in-person and online worship.

—**KAY KOTAN**, coach, church consultant, speaker and author and the Director of the Center for Equipping Vital Congregations for the Susquehanna Conference of The United Methodist Church

In his new book, *Both/And*, Jason Moore has given church leaders a powerful resource we will all reference again and again as we move forward in ministry. I agree with Jason that the church today finds itself in a Great Commission moment. How we respond today will echo for generations. Throughout this book you will find practical tools, concepts, and ideas your church will be able to use right away—AND come back to as our environment continues to change around us. This resource is a wonderful companion to Jason's outstanding webinars, coaching, and training. Pick up a copy for everyone in your church who services in any area of worship.

—**KEN WILLARD**, PCC, Director of Congregational Vitality, West Virginia Conference of The United Methodist Church

For two decades Jason Moore has been at the forefront of church and technology. I can't think of a better person to guide you and your church into our present future—a digitally connected world where the kingdom is expanding further and further into physical and digital places.

—**LUKE EDWARDS**, Associate Director of Church Development, Western NC Conference and Author of *Becoming Church: A Trail Guide for Starting Fresh Expressions*

Jason Moore's *Both/And* is a must-read for any church, pastor, and layperson who desires to reach people in our day and age. Moore delivers practical advice for churches no matter their size, shape, and DNA. *Both/And* is accessible material that can be accessed and implemented at any level. Jason's years of experience and love for the local church shines through *Both/And*. Any reader will be highly motivated and encouraged to reach more people for Christ.

—**ROSARIO PICARDO**, consultant, coach, co-pastor of Mosaic Church and Director of United Theological Seminary's Pohly Center for Supervision and Leadership Formation

Two years into dealing with COVID-19, we're still navigating how to best do in-person & online worship in a way that honors and engages both audiences. In Both/And, my friend Jason shows the Church how to rethink online worship in a way that's not a have-to, but a get-to. Pandemic or no pandemic, God challenges us to reach people wherever they're at, and online continues to be that place to reach people. Every church and church leader can benefit from reading Jason's words and putting them into practice as we continue to be the Church, in-person and online.

—**ADAM WEBER**, lead pastor of Embrace Church, author of *Love Has A Name*, and host of *The Conversation* podcast

A must-read for anyone wanting to understand the dramatic shift that the church made into digital ministry during covid-19 and how crucial it is for the church to continue to lean into "both/and" ministry moving forward. This book is a phenomenal resource for the church that is and the church that will be!

— **REV. RACHEL GILMORE**, church planter, author, coach, missional consultant at Central UMC in Phoenix, Arizona, co-founder of Intersect: a Co-Planting Network, Advisory Committee for the Fresh Expressions House of Studies at United Theological Seminary

Jason Moore's new book is a must-have powerhouse resource for every church of any size or setting. Its pages overflow with both new "golden nuggets" of learning as well as practical application guidance, birthed from Jason's personal experiences as trainer and consultant for countless churches across the country. Highly recommend!

—**REV. SUE NILSON KIBBEY**, Director, Bishop Bruce Ough Innovation Center, United Theological Seminary

invite
PRESS

BOTH/AND

MAXIMIZING HYBRID WORSHIP EXPERIENCES

FOR IN-PERSON AND ONLINE ENGAGEMENT

JASON MOORE

Plano, Texas

BOTH/AND: MAXIMIZING HYBRID WORSHIP EXPERIENCES
FOR IN-PERSON AND ONLINE ENGAGEMENT

Copyright 2022 by Jason Moore

This book is printed on acid-free, elemental chlorine-free paper.

Paperback: 978-1-953495-23-5;
eBook: 978-1-953495-24-2

22 23 24 25 26 27 28 29 30 31—10 9 8 7 6 5 4 3 2 1

MANUFACTURED in the UNITED STATES of AMERICA

I dedicate this book to my friend, Ohio State Trooper, Lt. Brian K. Aller. Covid-19 took this incredible father, husband, and member of our community too soon.

TABLE OF CONTENTS

RESOURCES

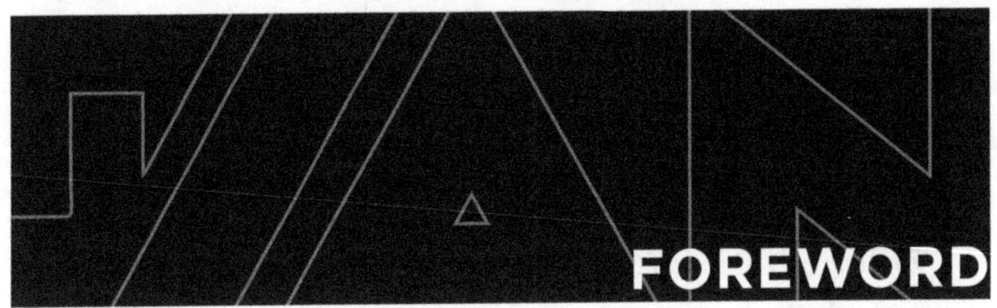

FOREWORD

Jason Moore is about to remind you that we are living in a Great Commission moment. He opens this important book by grounding it in a Biblical passage that has historically been central to the Church's fundamental purpose in the world (Matt 28: 18-20). In essence, Jason picks up where Matthew leaves off, with Jesus' closing commission.

In that final post-resurrection appearance, Jesus stands on a Galilea mountain in all his glorious, wound-bearing, death-conquering fullness, and sends the disciples out to be a continuation of his own life in the world. He authorizes and sends them, instructing them that as they go along the journey of life, they should make disciples, little mini-Christ's, who live, walk, talk, and love like Jesus. This commission is global in scope, encompassing all peoples and the entire world.

It will require them to cross boundaries, geographic, political, cultural, and religious.

This is what those first disciples did. They left the sense of comfort and familiarity behind. Courageously, they moved into places they had never even dreamed of before. They learned new customs, new languages, new ways of communicating, new ways of forming community, and new ways to worship. In many cases they experienced rejection and resistance, from both inside the community, and outside of it. Some of them were imprisoned, humiliated, and even executed as they sought to faithfully fulfill Jesus' instructions.

From that time until now, Christians have been crossing boundaries, sharing the gospel, and exploring new forms to worship the living God. In every generation, time, and place, followers of Jesus must find faithful ways to do this. Boundary crossing worship takes place in new and ever-changing contexts.

In the 21st Century, the new boundary to be crossed is a digital one. As Fred Rogers once famously said, "The space between the television set and the viewer is holy ground. A lot happens—a lot happens—there." Indeed, what if the space between our screens is holy ground? What if find ourselves on a new missional frontier, in a Great Commission moment?

We live in a time coined "The Digital Age," a period starting in the 1970s in which the personal computer became widely available. In the 1980s computer access combined with the Internet in the 1990s facilitated the dramatic proliferation of digital devices. In the 2010s, the smartphone revolution, essentially placed a supercomputer into the pocket of billions of human beings. The amalgamation of this mobile technology created a new hyper-connected social web.

The distanced contact made possible by the first telegraph sent on May 24th, 1844, has now evolved into a global means of interactive, multimodal, mass self-communication. Distanced contact allows simultaneity introduced in social relationships at a distance. This has not only revolutionized how we communicate; it has changed how human beings think, work, fall in love, live, and worship.

We must now see the online space as a new kind of third place. In the same way that cities provide opportunity for encounter in onsite space, the digital ecosystem facilitates distanced contact in the space of flows. Just as a city is a built environment that both facilitates and limits the movement of people through a space, the web is a digitally built environment, that facilitates and limits the movement of people through a virtual ecosystem. Connections, passions, and relationships are formed in the built environment of the cyberscape.

To say then that "virtual" is in some sense less "real" is a missional cul-de-sac. For many, the virtual space is no more or less real than the physical space that their body inhabits. For digital natives (those born with screens in their homes) social networks, such as Facebook, Twitter, and Pinterest, or Discord, Twitch, Second Life, and Friendster, constitute a very real part of our lives.

As Jason will show us, when the pandemic forced mandatory stay at home orders, every congregation suddenly had to figure out how to worship in this new space. To some degree, every church had to become a "digital" church overnight, when these mandatory quarantine precautions came forth. Whether we liked it or not, if we wanted to have a worship experience on Sunday morning, we had to figure out how to do it online.

Was the online worship offered by churches not real? When we attended the funerals of loved ones digitally was it somehow less real? When we communicated by FaceTime with loved ones locked down in care facilities were our interactions fake? These experiences may have been less sensory and immersive than in-person contact, but not less real. Jason will warn us not to abandon all the learnings, connections, and relationships during this disruptive season. We should not rush back into our sanctuaries, leaving the online frontier behind.

In the digital age, most people will have their first encounter with the church not by walking into our sanctuaries on Sunday morning, but by whatever kind of presence we offer in the online ecosystem. But does this mean what we do in our sanctuaries is useless or irrelevant? Absolutely not! Moore goes to great lengths to reflect on the essential truth communicated by Jesus in this parable:

"Neither is new wine put into old wineskins; otherwise, the skins burst, and the wine is spilled, and the skins are destroyed; but new wine is put into fresh wineskins, and so both are preserved" (Matt 9:17).

New wine goes through a fermentation process. In the molecular sense, the gaseous expansion and chemical transformation stretches, expands, and ultimately hardens the wineskin. You can't pour new wine into an already stretched and hardened skin; the fermentation process of the new wine would burst the skin. It's like Jesus is saying to his hearers, I've got this new wine I want to pour into you, this profuse grace, and unfailing love, this "good news for all people" (Lk 2:10). But if I tried to pour it into the rigidity of your thinking, your hardened religiosity, it would burst you!

The content of this good news is eternally true and consists of some fundamental ingredients. Those ingredients come in many flavors. But the delivery vehicle, the container is always changing. The forms of Christian worship have been changing ever since that first group of disciples descended that mountain in Galilee and started crossing boundaries. The forms of the church will continue to change, as the gospel, takes on flesh, and moves into the neighborhood (John 1).

This is true whether we are talking good old fashioned, cell swapping, molecule exchanging, face to face, flesh and blood community that "makes our joy complete" (2 John 12). Or the fresh exchange of pixels and distanced contact mediated through the multitude of digital flows in bits and bytes. Real people gather there too. For real community. And real worship.

Vintage wine needs vintage skins. Fresh wine needs fresh skins. The key to Jesus' teaching is found in one little word, "AND"… "and so both are preserved" (Matt 9:17).

On this new missional frontier, every single congregation will need to be a blended ecology of worship. Worship that is "gathered and scattered" "centered and dispersed" "attractional and missional" "digital and analog" "onsite and online." The key word for Jason, is the genius of "AND" and he will advocate here for diverse modes of worship living together in a synergistic way.

This both/and way allows us to rethink how we carry out the Great Commission. It provides us a fresh vision for how the church can be about our boundary crossing mission. Ultimately, it shows us how we can reach new people and invite them into a journey of following Jesus. So, get ready for an exciting journey onto a new missional frontier! On this adventure, Jason Moore is a trusted guide.

-Dr. Michael Adam Beck, pastor, professor, and author.
Director of the Fresh Expressions House of Studies at United Seminary,
Cultivator of Fresh Expressions Florida, and Director of ReMissioning
for Fresh Expressions US. MichaelAdamBeck.com

ACKNOWLEDGEMENTS

A book like this doesn't happen without a band of supporters, collaborators, cheerleaders, colleagues, and friends. While I'd like to thank each of them individually it would take an entire chapter to acknowledge them all one-by-one. Still, I want to thank several groups and individuals, because without them, this never would have come about.

First and foremost, my partner in life and my beloved bride, Michele Moore, manages our household and everything else in such a way I can do things like write books. I'm grateful for the sacrifices she and my kids have made that allow me to do what I do. I love you Michele, Ethan, and Madeline. Thank you.

This book and much of my work over 2020 and 2021 would not have happened if not for four people. Pastor Jeremy Scott was the spark that ignited the fire that became Both/And by asking me to secret worship his online service when the world shut down. With Jeremy's blessing and encouragement, the learnings from that consultation became an article that went viral. Gary Shockley saw that article, and the day after I posted it asked me to develop a webinar based on it. The following day, Ken Willard called with the same request and then went about helping me in numerous ways behind the scenes to make it a reality. That fall, Matt Burke (The Center for Congregations) commissioned my Both/And webinar after a brief conversation about my concerns for what would happen when churches went back in person while maintaining online worship. Thank you, Jeremy, Gary, Ken, and Matt. You changed the trajectory of my ministry.

From March of 2020 until fall of 2021, I've had nearly every single United Methodist Conference in the U.S.A, several ecumenical organizations, and a couple of seminaries host my Both/And training. The list of people that made these trainings possible is vast. Thank you to every conference leader and webinar host for your investment and trust in me. Thanks also to the attendees of these trainings for the ways you offered your learnings, thoughts, and feedback.

There were a group of twenty or thirty "beta testers" who attended my prototype webinars. They sat through the raw materials that became the trainings that led to this book. I can't thank you all enough for being there and helping me shape the content in real time as I was creating it.

You'll see "my friend," preceding names of pastors and leaders numerous times throughout the book. I want to thank every one of those individuals for sharing their stories and allowing me to tell them.

I've had the incredible privilege of coaching and consulting with almost two hundred leaders since the beginning of the pandemic. We've learned so much together. Thank you to each one of you who invested in me in this season. A large number of those leaders have participated in coaching relationships established through one of the five United Methodist Annual Conferences I've been privileged to be on retainer with in 2021. Thank you to Kelly Brown and Beth Ortiz of the East Ohio Conference, Dan Pezet and Rob Hutchinson of the Western North Carolina Conference, Craig Brown of the California-Nevada Conference, Gloria Fowler and Sam Hubbard of the Louisiana Conference, and Amy Ezell of the Arkansas Conference. It has been an enormous blessing to work with you and the churches you lead.

The team at Invite Press has been such a wonderful partner. I'm grateful for my longtime friend and former ministry partner Len Wilson for helping me bring this project to fruition. I want to say an especially heartfelt thanks to my editor Lori Wagner who helped me shape this into something I'm very proud of. She took it to the next level. Thanks to everyone else on the Invite team for supporting this work as well.

Thanks to Michael Beck for providing a wonderful foreword that sets the right tone for the book. You are an inspirational leader and I'm happy to know you.

There are a few individuals I want to name here that have had a very special role in my life during the development of this book. Rob Hutchinson, you've become a great friend and trusted sounding board. Thanks for always caring for me and being a great conversation partner as I explore Both/And ministry. Jon Ferguson, I so admired the work you did to make a Both/And reality possible at Stillwater. Your leadership and desire to lean into always making things better is inspiring. Andy Hill, you have been a great co-learner and fellow explorer in this unprecedented season. I appreciate you and our conversations so much. Ann Marie Carley, Tony Miltenberger, Tim Gossett, and Dan Roth, thanks for jumping in and helping me in the development of my Both/And trainings. From writing sections of my handbook to helping me troubleshoot and learn, your help was invaluable.

Finally, I want to thank you, the reader, for all of the hard work you've done throughout and beyond this pandemic. It's been so hard! I hope this book is helpful to you, and I thank you for picking it up.

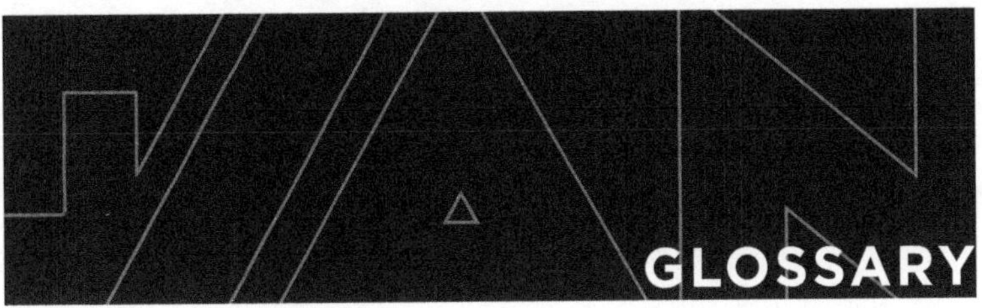

GLOSSARY

There are a few terms I'll be using throughout the book that I'd like to define here. First, we'll start with the title. You'll see lots of references to Both/And. I'll be using Both/And as a synonym for hybrid much of the time. When I refer to Both/And worship, I mean worship that is both in-person and online. Later in the book we're going to break that down into three different forms. I'll further define them in later chapters, but I'll preface them here:

PRE BOTH/AND WORSHIP

When I'm referring to this form, I mean worship that is prerecorded and/or pre-produced. This can be as simple as prerecording a sermon or other elements with a phone in one take, or as complicated as using multiple cameras, motion graphics, and complex editing. Pre Both/And worship also involves a separate experience of worship that is live with no cameras involved. In other words, this form involves planning one service and carrying it out in two ways: prerecorded and live in the room (with no streaming).

REAL TIME BOTH/AND WORSHIP

This form of worship is what many people first think of when they think of hybrid worship. This is livestreaming in the moment. This version assumes that you're doing worship in the room, and you have cameras broadcasting it in real time.

POST BOTH/AND WORSHIP

The final form I'll refer to is Post Both/And worship. This is worship that is offered live in-person and recorded as it's happening but is not streamed in real time. Post Both/And worship will be posted online later that day, week, or at some other designated time. Post-editing or post-production may be involved. Like Pre Both/And worship, this could be a simple one take recording from a phone or a more advanced edit.

INTRODUCTION

"All authority in heaven and on earth has been given to me. Go therefore and make disciples of all nations, baptizing them in the name of the Father and of the Son and of the Holy Spirit, and teaching them to obey everything that I have commanded you. And remember, I am with you always, to the end of the age."

Matthew 28:18 – 20, NRSV

Jesus, in what we call the "Great Commission," lays out for us a lofty, yet relatively straight forward command, that we are to "make disciples of all nations" (Matt 28:19). From the earliest days of Jesus' ministry, and the church that formed out of it, to those who are living in this present time, the good news of the gospel remains vibrant, resonant, and powerful; however, the reception of and means by which we share the good news of Jesus Christ has changed radically.

Many shifts, some more dramatic than others, have occurred within the church. Other more recent shifts have emerged from cultural changes and circumstances that have either seeped into the church unknowingly or have forced the church kicking and screaming into the 21st century in order to survive. The impetus for every shift has been a significant change in technology. By technology, I mean the forms of communication used to convey Jesus' message to disciples inside and outside of the church. The historic progression from handwritten letters, to manuscripts, to the printing press, telegraph, telephone, radio, broadcast television, and internet has made it possible to continue to invite people into transformational experiences of worship for centuries. Today is no exception. In fact, worship today has the potential to be more powerful, connective, and resonant than ever before, if only churches will take advantage of their newest and best resource: the internet.

This book will take a look at worship today and will explore how technology and cultural phenomena, specifically the rapid growth of internet technology and the recent impact of the pandemic, have changed and will continue to change the way we do worship and experience Jesus, his message, and ultimately our means for carrying out the "great commission." In the book, I'll give you ideas, examples, and some innovative ways to re-imagine worship. I'll introduce to you new and important questions that need to be asked by churches and para-churches and suggest some possible ways of addressing those questions. Most of all, I will help you re-evaluate what it means to be the dynamic and vital church God imagined us to be in this time and place. We are living in tumultuous times. But often great discoveries, innovations, and impact can emerge from times like these, times that force us to ask ourselves tough questions about who we are and how we see our future. How can we embrace technology in ways that enhance worship and yet keep our church grounded and unified? How can we welcome new forms of worship and yet not betray the traditions and rituals we hold dear? How can we value our past and our current congregation and yet welcome new kinds of worshipers and inquisitive online Christians? How can we value our in-person connections and yet connect and resonate with those beyond our walls? These do not have to be either/or questions. I hope to show you in fact throughout this book that these are both/and questions. Through embracing both online and in-person (or hybrid) worship, we can ultimately create more dynamic worship experiences, deepen our identity, broaden the church's scope, and enhance people's experience of Jesus in their lives. Let's grasp opportunity by the tail together and create the kind of powerful, life-altering worship experiences that change hearts and save lives. The future of the church is depending on you.

2020 marked a significant turning point for the future of the church. Regardless of when churches began offering online worship, the 2020 pandemic forced every church to immediately rethink its strategy for holding and leading worship. While many jumped online in a matter of days for the very first time, others who had been online for years still now had to grapple with how to create an experience of worship for people not gathered together in a physical space. Many churches recognized that not everything about the in-person experience translated to the experience at home. Others more-or-less went about business as usual, placing a camera in the back of the room and doing what they had typically done before the pandemic, only now they were streaming worship to an online audience.

But before conversing about methodology, I want to celebrate what's happened in the church over the course of 2020 and 2021. Whether a church had been online a decade before the pandemic hit, or whether it jumped online just after the world shut down, there is much to celebrate. Every effort has been worthy – from the single smartphone streaming to Facebook Live, to three-camera setups running fancy software streaming to multiple platforms. The church, usually as slow-moving and change-resistant as a tortoise, has never been so malleable and has never moved so quickly. In the early days of the pandemic, it was as if we were witnesses to the present-day equivalent of Gutenberg firing up his press to make the Bible available to the masses for the first time. While Covid-19 brought about some very difficult losses: loss of life, financial hardship, and so on, it also forced change upon us in a way that opened worship and the church up to new people and possibilities in ways never before attempted.

I would venture to guess that most of us never expected mass participation in the offering of online worship to be one of the most effective ways to fulfill The Great Commission, but we're reaching more people now than ever before, because we are streaming worship to the masses. Over the course of 2020 and 2021, I've heard numerous stories of how church attendance has risen in congregations large and small. Some have reported that they are reaching double the attendees, and others have seen an increase as many as five times the number of attendees than had been participating prior to the pandemic. Christianity Today has been studying the data and estimates that online attendance has tripled in 2020/2021.[1] And while this isn't the story for everyone (we'll get to why that may be), it's an exciting time to be the church.

Most houses of worship ended in-person gatherings of worship around the second or third weekend of March 2020 due to the nearly nationwide pandemic shut down. This meant a large number (very likely the majority) of churches, who had never been online before, needed to find a way to

1. Enoch Hill, Jason Long, and Cole Serfass, "Church Decline and Recovery During COVID-19," *Christianity Today*, May 17, 2021, https://www.christianitytoday.com/edstetzer/2021/may/church-decline-and-recovery-during-covid-19.html.

offer a worship experience that wasn't reliant on a physical gathering with leaders and participants. With only days to react, pastors and leaders turned to their smartphones, tablet devices, and video cameras to stream worship.

The approach taken by many new to online worship mimicked the early days of film. Prior to the advent of film cameras, opera and theater were two of the most popular forms of entertainment. When the new technology of film cameras came about, it was only natural that many early films were simply stage plays captured on camera.

Len Wilson writes about this in *The Wired Church 2.0*:

> Early film imitated theater, locking down the camera in the best seat of the house and staying wide all the time to capture the entire stage. The first revolutionary director was D. W. Griffith, who in 1908 introduced two incredible techniques: a close-up of the protagonist and editing between two scenes.[2]

Necessity was the catalyst for the shifting of the worship paradigm in 2020. Without much time to develop strategies, a lot of churches just did what they'd always done. They conducted a worship service that looked a lot like what had happened every other week prior, only now with a camera broadcasting the entire (empty) room. There was an almost utilitarian approach to the process of streaming worship in the earliest days of the pandemic. Without meaning to, some failed to recognize that one medium doesn't translate one-to-one into another. Some saw (and continue to see) online worship as a necessary evil, and many lamented (and continue to lament) having to move to this new format. But this isn't the first time we've been through the pains of change where worship is concerned. In his book *Perimeters of Light: Biblical Boundaries for the Emerging Church*, author Ed Stetzer outlines the conflict that has existed in the church over its life surrounding music. Among other things, he writes about the controversies that span from the 200s to the 2000s around everything from instrumentation (flutes and organs) to music with a beat.

The casualties of the "worship wars" are buried across the expanse of the church throughout time, but in this instance, we didn't have time to

2. Len Wilson, *The Wired Church 2.0* (Nashville, TN: Abingdon Press, 2008), 24.

pick up weapons and go to war. We had to shift strategies right away so that ministry could continue when shelter-in-place orders were issued.

In pre-pandemic worship, for those who were already committed to some form of online worship, those who were ahead of the curve, strategy was not so much a concern. Worship most often began with a welcome to the room. We'd enthusiastically say to everyone gathered right in front of our eyes something like, "Good morning and welcome to worship. We're so glad you're here today." And then we'd turn to the camera, give a quick little ten second nod to the online audience and say, "And welcome to those of you who are worshiping with us online today, too." From there, we'd pretty much go back to talking to the room for the rest of the experience, and in most online experiences, we'd never talk directly to the audience worshiping at home again. Now, at the time (pre-pandemic), this seemed to us perfectly acceptable. We had very few models for directly communicating with those at home. And we really didn't count them as a major or vital part of the congregation. They were in a sense "outliers" in our eyes, those who avoided committing to what we deemed true membership or true commitment. We liked that they were tuning in, but they were not our central focus. When Covid-19 shut us all down – for those who were already online – our strategy completely changed. Suddenly, we went from looking only at and addressing the people in the room, to looking directly into the camera and offering worship in such a way that people on the other side of that camera would feel like they were a part of it. Not only did we look at the camera, but we also began adapting how we planned worship for people not gathered in a physical space. Our outliers had become our primary focus group.

I believe those who worshiped online prior to the pandemic could feel that change in our attention. We woke them up to what it felt like to be talked to directly, and we invited them to be participants in the worship experience.

But what about those who were newcomers to online worship? Nearly all of those who took worship online for the first time during the pandemic learned quickly to look directly at the camera. They didn't have the challenge of whether to address the camera or the room, because there was no one in the space.

Whether when this book is released or sometime in the near future, the Covid-19 pandemic will hopefully be over. I pray that with this book in your hands, your return to in-person worship can commence and the restrictions we've all experienced throughout 2020 and 2021 might be an uncomfortable memory. With that stated, I believe we are living through one of the most critical moments in the life of the modern church as we consider what's next. Even as I'm writing this book, I'm beginning to see the resolve, passion, excitement, and recognition of what this season has meant to the church fade. People are already asking, "Can we drop this online worship thing now?" In the conclusion to this book, I'll share multiple reasons why we should continue Both/And indefinitely.

My intent as you read though this book is to challenge you to think through or rethink your approach to worship and what it means to imagine a truly hybrid worship. People throw the words "hybrid worship" around pretty haphazardly. Truly hybrid worship – worship where everyone feels they're a part of it – is worship where everyone feels like they're the primary audience.

If we're not careful, we are likely to lose all of the momentum we've gained over the years of the pandemic. If we're not careful, without an intentional strategy, I think one of two things is very likely to happen as we go back to doing in-person worship while continuing online worship. The first is that after spending so long worshiping online, we might be so in the habit of talking to the camera that we'll inadvertently turn the room into a studio audience providing the claps, laughs, and voices for the songs we sing. Think Saturday Night Live and how the actors play to the camera. The people are there to react and give the performers an audience. In this scenario, we will favor the online audience, and the people in the room will become secondary. The second possibility – the one I think is most likely – is that when we have people back in our worship spaces, we'll turn the entirety of our attention to them. This will make those worshiping online from home (or wherever they may be) feel as if they're observers or spectators of an experience they're no longer a part of. We will unintentionally re-marginalize our newest and perhaps most vital disciples and decimate our greatest and most promising future church potential.

Some of those online participants have only ever known us online. Perhaps they haven't returned yet, or perhaps for a variety of reasons, they prefer online to in-person worship. At the end of the day, nobody wants to be an afterthought. For the church to remain open, vital, and for it to continue to expand its horizons and scope, it's imperative that we begin now to strategize about what I call Both/And worship. What worship looks like in our next season of ministry will define the future of the church.

If we want to build on the incredible momentum we've gained in 2020 and 2021, we cannot go backwards. We have to instead dream about what the next iteration of ministry looks like in a post pandemic world. The worship we do next shouldn't look exactly like it did before the pandemic, and it shouldn't look exactly like it did during the pandemic either. I hope you'll read on with an open mind, as we explore together what the rites and rituals for this new paradigm of worship might look like.

PART I
THE NEW PARADIGM

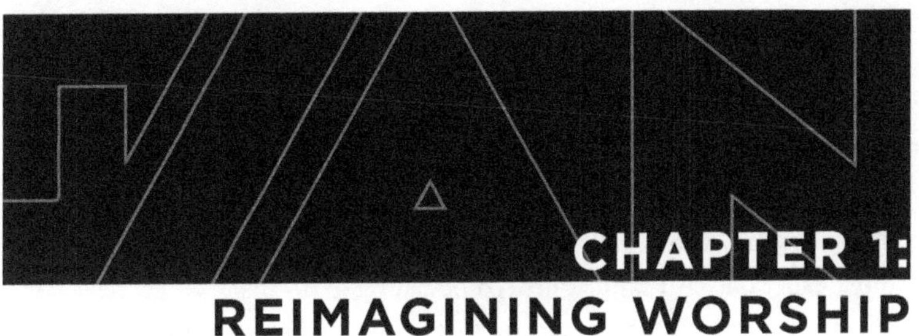

CHAPTER 1: REIMAGINING WORSHIP

"Churches cancel Sunday service, move online amid coronavirus outbreak"[1]

Headlines like the one above from Fox News were common across the internet and newspapers alike in the final weeks of March 2020. It was unfathomable that services would not be offered in-person for Easter that year, and churches scrambled to figure out how to make one of the highest holy days of the church year happen without a building. Those already in the practice of streaming worship online had a bit of a head start, but every church would have to reimagine worship if they truly wanted to be effective in reaching those already in the fold and those who might casually happen upon a church's worship service on their Facebook timeline.

The second week of March 2020, a pastor friend of mine, Jeremy Scott, reached out to me in what seemed to be a bit of a panic. In 2019, I had flown out to his Denver area church to conduct a "secret worshiper" consultation. Secret worshiping is sort of like secret shopping, except I'm not there to buy anything. I'm there just to offer the outsider's perspective. This sort of makes me a "professional church visitor."

The process starts with an audit of a church's website, followed by an in-person visit to experience firsthand what a guest would experience. Extensive notes are taken from parking lot into the building. Careful attention is paid to signage, hospitality teams, and systems, children's ministry spaces, and check-in process, and so much more. In worship, I listen for guest friendly language, try to identify unspoken rituals, am aware of how

1. Caleb Parke, "Churches Cancel Sunday Service, Move Online Amid Coronavirus Outbreak," Fox News, March 13, 2020, https://www.foxnews.com/us/coronavirus-update-church-sunday-service-online.

seamless transitions are, critique the preaching, music, liturgy, and worship order, and look for anything else that might exclude or confuse a newcomer.

When the call began, Jeremy said, "Jason, we implemented pretty much everything you recommended in your report from last year. The changes you suggested have made a real difference, but they just shut down our in-person worship. We're online only now. Can you 'secret worship' our online experience?" I said, "Sure. I'd be happy to do that." A few days later, I sat in on his service from the comfort of my couch in an attempt to fully engage in the same way I would if I were in the building.

Jeremy is a gifted leader, a great preacher, and has a great team surrounding him. As happens every time I offer a consultation of this type, I identified some things that could use some tweaks for the season we were entering at the time. My notes that day filled the fronts and backs of two 8.5x11 sheets of paper. From the glowing affirmation I offered, to a carefully considered critique of the online experience, I had a lot to share with Jeremy and his team. What I recognized in both experiencing this worship and writing the report, was that with no in-person option to participate in, things were going to have to look different with online worship moving forward. Jeremy was online prior to the pandemic; this wasn't brand new for him. He was an early adopter. But he had never had to depend solely on an online experience.

When Jeremy's service was complete, I continued scrolling through my Facebook feed to see what others were doing. On that day in late March, my feed was so completely overtaken by streaming worship, I could hardly believe it. Pastors and churches I'd known for years, who had no real online presence, were doing worship with their smartphones, laptops, and whatever else they could cobble together to stream worship to their congregations. In many of them I noticed a pattern. They had embraced a new way of delivering worship by streaming it online, but the worship they were serving up was being done as if people were still in the room. To be clear, there was no one in the room to talk to.

As I read over my notes for Jeremy, I quickly realized that the feedback I'd be sharing with him could be beneficial to other churches who were also trying to navigate this new form of worship we'd all been thrust into. With his blessing, I adapted my notes into a short article I called "5 Things to Consider Before This Weekend's Online Worship Stream." I posted the article (the lessons of which will be sprinkled throughout this book in more complete form), and it went viral. As the shares, comments, and private messages came in, I received an email from one of my longtime friends, colleagues, and collaborators, Gary Shockley. Gary had read the article and asked me if I could turn it into a webinar for the Susquehanna Conference of The United Methodist Church. Gary serves as the director of Equipping Vital Churches for his region, and he too was looking for ways to help churches re-imagine worship during the pandemic.

Having only ever participated in one webinar that I was not responsible for running or planning, I asked for a couple of days to explore the possibilities. The following day another friend, Ken Willard, who has a very similar role in the West Virginia Conference of The United Methodist Church, called with the same request: "I'd like a webinar based on that post Jason. Can you do that?" I said, "I'm working on it."

Both of these friends helped me think through and flesh it all out. I began to fill a whiteboard with ideas, collect stories from my friends in the trenches, make phone calls, watch more online worship, and explore technology options, and I ultimately decided that I could indeed offer a webinar on this topic. "Telling the Old Story in a New Time: Best Practices for Online Worship and Beyond in a Physically Distanced World" was the title I gave this new training. Days after announcing that the training was a go on social media, I received invitations from fourteen United Methodist conferences to present the material live to each of their respective areas via a Zoom webinar. Everyone was hungry for material on how to do worship in a non-physical way, which was the sole focus of this training. Oh, and everyone wanted it before Easter, which made for two very long weeks of two and three trainings a day. The webinar included conversations about how to reimagine worship in multiple forms, including drive-in worship, streaming worship (in multiple forms), telephonic worship (the use of phones to broadcast worship to the less technically savvy), and analog worship (CDs, DVDs, paper, and other physical media for those not tech-savvy).

I talked about the importance of building community, how to do hospitality online, and had some brief conversations about licensing and copyright. We'll come back to those topics a little later. My hope was to help people see Covid-19 and the discontinuance of in-person worship as an opportunity to reach three audiences:

The Committed - These are the folks who were just waiting for you to tell them where to show up online and they'd be there.

This group is the group we tend to think about the most.

The Disconnected – These people may have left the "big C" church, or your church. They may be more open to returning than ever before given the pandemic, as well as the racial and political tensions that exist in the world today.

This group gets some of our attention, but we don't have to change up our language all that much when we consider they have some indoctrination into the church.

Those Seeking – This group is made up of people who may have some church memory or no church memory at all and those who are seeking spiritual and relational connection.

Much of our language, rituals, and common practices may be completely foreign to them. These people may be more open now than ever before to the church because of the pandemic and all of the perils it brought with it.

This is the group we often completely overlook when it comes to streaming worship online. For this group, we have to adapt our language and walk people through our rituals, customs, and practices.

Everything about how worship was received and how people participated changed when we left the building. Because of social media, people could accidentally "show up" to worship. Maybe it was in a Facebook watch party (a feature now discontinued) or through a link shared on a timeline. Maybe it was a YouTube suggested video, or a creative hashtag that led to the opportunity to experience worship. Whatever the case, reimagining worship for a new audience was critical when church went online.

Around the time I had conducted my thirtieth training, some churches began dabbling with the idea of reopening in limited numbers. Others had already returned to in-person worship. The words "hybrid worship" were commonly being used to describe the worship taking place at this time, worship that was offered both in-person and online at the same time.

While hybrid worship may have been the intent, the reality of that worship in many settings was simply to stream what was happening in the room with little to no regard for the online audience. Yet, truly hybrid worship is worship where no one feels like an afterthought; not the people in the room, nor the people at home. The ethos of truly hybrid worship must be rooted in equal concern for BOTH in-person worshipers AND those who are participating in the digital space.

FROM BOOK TO FILM

One of the ways I've been framing the conversation about hybrid worship is to think about how stories are adapted from book form to film form. In book form, stories are rich and complex. Narrative arcs play out in deeper, more nuanced ways with greater opportunity to explore character, settings, and plot. A book's structure is less constrained than the traditional three-act format of films. Most books that are made into films take a significant time investment to read, much more than that of a film. Storylines that support a 400-page book cannot possibly fit into a two-hour movie. One script page equals one minute of film, requiring approximately 110 script pages for a feature film.[2] This means a lot of cutting is required to make a book into a film. When a book is adapted into a film, numerous story issues must be overcome in order to capture the essence of that story in its new form. The stories must be consolidated and adapted, limits of the new medium must be embraced, and narratives must be reimagined. The same is true when moving from in-person physical gatherings of worship to online digital forms of worship.

The beauty of this last year (whether or not we've been intentional) is that our story – what we do in worship to connect people to Jesus Christ – has been told in a new way for a new time, and in many cases for new people.

When a book becomes a film, its story is also opened up to a much broader audience. A 2014 BBC news article revealed that researchers found 75% of men would opt for the big screen version of a story, while 30% admitted they had not picked up a book since they were at school.[3] Many people will never walk into a bookstore to buy a book, nor will they go to the library to check it out. When a book is made into a film, many more people will see the movie than will read the book. Movies have a far-reaching impact. While the written word was once the primary means by which we experienced everything from news to entertainment, movies and television have increasingly become the most popular form of consuming content in our society.

---

2. Jeanne Veillette Bowerman, "Take Two: How to Adapt a Book Into a Screenplay," *Writer's Digest*, June 26, 2019, https://www.writersdigest.com/write-better-fiction/take-two-how-to-adapt-a-book-into-a-screenplay.

3. BBC News, "Men 'giving up' on books to watch films or go online," BBC.com, April 16, 2014, https://www.bbc.com/news/entertainment-arts-27056440.

Yet, when the adaptation of a story from book to film occurs, and the film is good, some percentage of its audience will then buy the book, so they can experience the more complete version of the story. This is often true for me.

When Steven Spielberg's *Jurassic Park* debuted in theaters, I was a junior in high school. That industry-redefining film and its use of cutting-edge computer graphics completely blew me away. At that time in my life, I was not much of a reader. It was only after the film came out that I learned that it was based on a Michael Crichton book. Once I learned of the book, I checked it out from the library and consumed it in a matter of days. The same was true for my favorite movie of all time, *The Shawshank Redemption*. It was only after I fell in love with the film that I learned that its genesis was a Stephen King short story. I bought the book immediately.

I have not purchased a Marvel comic since I was in eighth or ninth grade. Sure, the MCU has reimagined some of the stories for the big screen, but I've experienced those stories and have invested time and money in them. Without the Marvel Cinematic Universe, I'd likely have never experienced those stories.

A similar phenomenon can happen with worship too. When we do the hard work of reimagining worship for a new medium and we tell our old story in a new way for a new time, some who experience it will be so moved by the story that they'll want to experience it in person. In other words, some may be ready for the "book version" and will be drawn to our physical gatherings of worship. This is already happening in many churches. I've heard numerous stories in the first six months of 2021 about how churches are seeing more first-time visitors than ever before, most of whom came after attending online.

But what if they don't come in person? What if they only ever want to attend online? These are questions and concerns I hear expressed all the time by critics of online worship. While I do not advocate replacing in-person worship with online worship altogether – what we experience in relationship building and physical contact is hard to replace online – I do think that well-crafted and strategic expressions of worship can be equally transformational. Those who experience the transformational power of Jesus Christ in their lives through online worship know that this form of worship can have an incredible impact. Some people may be reconnecting with their faith after having left the church long ago. Many shut-ins describe the most powerful expressions of worship they have ever experienced. Those who have been shunned from the church may now be able to worship in a way that feels safe. For many of these and others online worship has so much to offer. I've heard reports of positive experiences in online worship playing out in churches across the globe. The bottom line is, if online worship is making a difference, does it matter if some people ever pass through our physical doors?

NEW WINESKINS

I see what's happened in 2020/2021 as a "new wineskins moment." Jesus said, "Neither do people pour new wine into old wineskins. If they do, the skins will burst; the wine will run out and the wineskins will be ruined. No, they pour new wine into new wineskins, and both are preserved" (Matthew 9:17 NIV). Covid-19 forced us to find a new wineskin in a time where it would have been impossible to taste the wine. Online worship is a new wineskin. The Good News hasn't changed. What's changed is how we wrap it up and deliver it. Now, let's be honest, the vast majority of the time, viewers of film adaptations who started with the book do not like the movie as much as they liked the book. Except for a small handful of exceptions such as *Charlie and the Chocolate Factory*, *Jurassic Park*, and *Forrest Gump*,[4] movies usually pale in comparison to their companion books.

In the same way, many of us don't love online worship as much as we love in-person worship. Some have merely tolerated it. Many times over the last year, I've heard people say that they'll be glad when the pandemic is over, so they don't have to do worship online anymore. I cringe every time I hear this. We're having far greater impact than ever before as we're telling our story to those who may never have experienced it before. And yet, many would rather go backward to what was familiar rather than forward into what's exciting and new, vital, and evangelistic.

I was leading a consultation at a wonderful church in Wisconsin who had hired me to help them build a robust Both/And strategy. It was early June of 2021, and this church had only re-opened for in-person worship a few weeks before my visit. During a visioning session I was leading with

4. "From Fiction to Film: Exploring Perceptions of Book-to-Screen Adaptations," *SuperSummary*, accessed September 23, 2021, https://www.supersummary.com/from-fiction-to-film/.

the leaders, a very well-intentioned gentleman came to me during a break and very innocently asked me if their church could discontinue online worship. The reason he cited for asking the question was that they were already about ninety percent back in person now. I promptly gave him a list of reasons why ending the online worship experience wasn't a good decision. He turned to me and said, "Okay. I guess that makes sense." I wasn't sure he was convinced. The very next day I sat in the back pew of the sanctuary taking notes during worship for my "secret worshiper report." I filled up six pages on this particular Sunday. When the service concluded, the woman sitting next to me leaned over and said, "Are you a blogger or something? I saw you taking a lot of notes." I said, "No, I'm here consulting with your church. I'm helping you build strategies for your online and in-person worship." She lit up with a huge smile when I told her this. She went on to say, "We're brand new here. We found this church because they had a Good Friday service online – one of the only ones we could find. We were so impressed with that service that we watched the following Sunday and every Sunday after that. When they began offering in-person worship again a few weeks ago, we came that week and haven't missed a Sunday since then. We just moved to the area, so I don't know if we would have found this church if not for their online worship. Tell them they're doing a good job."

During a post-worship luncheon with the team, I shared this story with the gentleman who had asked me the question about canceling online worship the day before. He jokingly responded, "I'm convinced!"

The desire to move away from online and hybrid worship is understandable. It's the film version of our book and it's a hard pill for some to swallow. To compare in-person worship to online worship is simply unfair. We've had centuries to work out our theology, polity, and methodology for in-person worship. We know how to do it well – like the back of our hand. We've only had just about a year to consider what any of these things look like for online worship. As much as we'd like it to, what we do in-person doesn't always translate to online.

In a conference call, a United Methodist Conference leader from Iowa, Lanette Plambeck, and I were discussing this unfair comparison. Lanette pointed out something I hadn't considered about online and hybrid worship. She said, "We have yet to develop our rites and rituals for online worship and how they play out." She is right. We jumped in headfirst because we had to. Sure, some churches were online before the pandemic, but the majority thrust online hadn't wrestled with the theological implications of online worship, how sacramental life and other rites and rituals would be affected by the inability to gather in person. There wasn't time to build a strategy and enter into a prolonged debate about what could and couldn't or should and shouldn't be done.

In my tribe, The United Methodist Church, there was no uniform approach for how to offer sacraments like communion. I learned very quickly in my Both/And trainings (offered to nearly every United Methodist Conference in the U.S.) that I had to avoid blanket statements. In some conferences, online communion was forbidden. In others it was okay. Some Bishops did not allow for singing. Others left it up to the church. Even now, many have not stopped to really think about what rites and rituals belong in online worship and how they should be carried out for those not in the physical space. My hope is that as you read this book, you'll begin to develop those rites and rituals and decide how they should play out in your worship services.

Not everything in our in-person gatherings of worship translate to the online experience. This reality is really hard to accept for some. Many things about in-person worship simply don't work online. That's why our in-person story (book) must be reconceptualized for an online audience (film).

RESONANT WORSHIP

When it comes to online worship, the environment people are participating in, be it their living room, a hotel room, nursing home, or what have you, is less controlled. The opportunity for distraction is dramatically higher. Doorbells, coffee makers, pets, telephones, living room décor, and just about anything else can get in the way of the online experience, and focus becomes much more difficult. A church's worship center, sanctuary, or auditorium is a much more controlled environment. From lighting, to sacred symbols, windows, and woodwork, to smoke machines, LED lights, and screens, everything that is placed in the room is there to enhance the experience.

The in-person space, how it's arranged, and what's in it, is an advantage that you cannot fully benefit from online. The energy of the crowd cannot be replicated at home either. Yet those kinds of experiences all make us feel something when we worship. Without the symbols and the communal experience, some things do not translate from the church building to the experience we have at home sitting on our couches. So how do we energize and create resonant worship in the online format?

In the fall of 2020, I was invited to speak at a conference for digital church planters. I was among a team of speakers that included the incomparable and incredible Nona Jones. If you are not aware of Nona's work yet, it's time you know Nona. Her book, *From Social Media to Social Ministry: A Guide to Digital Discipleship*, is a gold mine of great insights about how to do ministry online. Among other things, Nona is the pastor of a church in Florida, but she is also the Director of Faith-Based Partnerships at Facebook. I loved sitting in on her session about doing worship online.

Nona gave some great advice about what the length of online worship should be, all based on the data they've been acquiring and studying at Facebook. Her advice was to, "Keep it tight. Keep it interesting. Keep it engaging. And don't go longer than 25-35 minutes."[5] She went on to say that at Facebook, as they continue to study the data, they've found that 40 minutes is the threshold where many viewers start to drop off. She advised a maximum length of 40 minutes for online expressions of worship. If that number is alarming, take heart. In a later chapter, I'm going to tell you how you can continue with whatever length you've done in in-person worship prior to the pandemic while still following Nona's advice.

Since March of 2020, I've led about 150 webinars on the topic of online and hybrid worship. This represents a sampling of over 15,000 leaders. In every training, I've asked participants how long their in-person worship was prior to the pandemic. The overwhelming majority of folks told me that pre-pandemic service length was around an hour to a little over an hour in length. Of course, cultural context is a factor that must be considered. Some participants offered worship at double that length, while others came in well under that. After eighteen months of observation, listening to what leaders were seeing, and my own experiences, I came to the conclusion that one hour was too long for online worship; we must consolidate the experience. Those who participate online just don't experience worship in the same way as they do when they're in the building.

Now, you may be reading these words thinking, "Jason, this doesn't match my experience. My people will watch for the entire hour or more

5. Nona Jones, "Digital Church Planter Training," UMCDiscipleship.org/DCPT, August 4-Sept 8, 2020.

at my church and they'll watch from prelude to closing music." That may very well be true. I'd never argue with your experience or what the data shows. If that statement does represent your experience, I'd invite you to consider that the key words in that sentence are, "my people." Yes, your people probably will tune in for the entirety of the experience, no matter the length. In 2020, things changed. We've shifted the way we deliver worship from one where people come to us at the time and space that we appoint (our building) to an approach where we take worship to them on their turf (online), where they can watch from wherever they want, whenever they want. What's even more disconcerting for worship planners today is that participants can now fast forward to the parts they want to see and skip the parts that don't appeal to them. As we continue to reimagine worship in the future, we'll have to give some thought to how we design worship in order to keep people engaged throughout.

We must consider that we have more eyes and ears on worship than ever before as a result of the pandemic. We cannot assume the same things we once did about people's eagerness to show up at our buildings each week. People who may never have come to church before are showing up online. They have no connection to our rituals and practices, and they don't love us the way we love each other. Without any buy-in or good will already established, we must consider that when it comes to online worship, shorter is better.

The longer a service goes, the harder it is to stay focused. According to a 2020 study conducted by the Barna Group, "67 percent of those who've only attended once or twice during the pandemic admit their attention wanes in online services." That same study also found that "more than one-third of adults who've attended church and engaged with online services during the pandemic (36%) say they have trouble focusing during said services."[6]

There are a number of factors that affect how people participate in worship and why we must consolidate the online experience.

In May of 2020, just a few months into the pandemic, blogger Eric Geiger conducted a Twitter poll to gather some data about online worship length. What he found was fascinating.

Eric explains the parameters of his poll:

---

6. Barna Group, *Six Questions About the Future of the Hybrid Church Experience*, (E-Book, published January 1, 2020), 7.

> There were three options for response in terms of length of service compared to "back in the day when we used to meet with people physically in the same room:" shorter, longer, or the same. More than 500 pastors responded and the overwhelming response (74%) was the services are shorter. A few brave souls (2.4%) are having longer services and the rest (24%) have worship services that are essentially the same length.[7]

This lines up with the anecdotal data that I've collected over the course of my webinars. Many attendees of my Both/And webinar have said their worship has been shortened to 30 to 45 minutes.

Eric goes on to share several reasons why online worship should be shortened:

> **1. Leaders are responding to "screen fatigue."**
> People are growing exhausted with the amount of time spent in front of a screen, whether on Zoom calls, group texts, or Google hangouts, and are experiencing screen fatigue. As church leaders are hearing of this fatigue, some are responding with briefer worship services.
>
> **2. Some worship service elements are missing.**
> Baptisms, communion, and times of greeting are not occurring in online only worship services, so service times are shorter even if the length of the message and the music remains the same.
>
> **3. Less interaction (less reading the room) reduces teaching time.**
> A sermon with the same word count and the same speaker will be shorter when there is no one in the room. I know this personally! When teaching to a live audience, you inevitably respond more. You pause for laughter. You double down on a point. You sense and respond to the room. All of that is gone when staring at a camera, and the sermon will be shorter unless you are adding more content.
>
> **4. Cultural norms for watching.**
> Shows on Netflix and other streaming platforms have trained the attention span of our people, and some church leaders are responding to that reality. A regular episode is less than an hour.

7. Eric Geiger, "5 Reasons 'Church at Home' Worship Service Times are Shorter," Ericgeiger.com, May 5, 2020, https://ericgeiger.com/2020/05/5-reasons-church-at-home-worship-service-times-are-shorter/.

> **5. Kids and junior high students are attending.**
> When a church that typically has kid's ministry that meets separate from the adults during a weekend worship service, the pastor who is teaching makes adaptions on services when there are more kids present (such as holidays). There are more kids present right now! They are just spread out through lots of living rooms rather than in one room.[8]

If we're trying to reach folk beyond our church walls, when we take into account the five areas Eric mentioned, we should all be striving to create resonant experiences with our online services by developing a consolidated, more engaging online worship experience.

ADAPT, ENERGIZE, AND ENGAGE!

In addition to consolidating our services, how do we create engaging, energizing, participatory online services that bring people closer to Jesus and include them in the worshiping experience, even though they are not in a room together? We need to look at the different facets of our worship services and re-imagine that experience online. Then, we must find ways to adapt those elements to an online format by thinking creatively about the way worshipers will experience and engage with online worship.

Music

One of the adaptations we must consider making for online experiences of worship that can be seen as controversial is that of singing less. The music portion of worship is one that doesn't always translate to the online experience. Worship in song is experienced so differently at home than it is in the physical space. From the acoustics in the room, to the contrast in sound quality from tiny speakers on a phone or TV, to the energy felt when singing in unison with a crowd, to that of sitting on a couch belting out lyrics with family, the experiences are just so very different.

In the trainings I've offered in 2020 and 2021, I've asked every group how many are fully participating in music at home. The overwhelming majority – like 85 or 90 percent - are telling me that they don't sing at all or only occasionally sing during online worship. Now, am I suggesting we drop singing from online worship? Absolutely not. Singing is an important

8. Eric Geiger, "5 Reasons 'Church at Home' Worship Service Times are Shorter."

act of worship. But we might consider consolidating the portion of worship where many aren't participating and may be skipping when watching on delay.

Before you assume I hate music or undervalue musicians and worship leaders, know that I'm a musician myself and have led worship in many services over the last several decades. I love music, but even I don't sing much when worshiping online. My wife participates more than I do, but neither of us are fully engaged during this time. And then there are my kids. There is nothing more difficult than keeping my teenage kids in front of the TV during this portion of worship. Neither of them want to sing in front of us or each other.

Of course, when you have extremely talented musicians, multi-camera set ups, fog machines, synchronized lights and so on, you might engage and retain people at a deeper level for a longer period of time. Few of us are at the level of Elevation Church, Northpointe Ministries, or other megachurches who are delivering high production value concert-like experiences.

With Both/And worship there are ways not to have to compromise the singing we do in person while still consolidating the online experience. We'll come back to that a bit later as we get into specific strategies. For purely online worship, shortened music sets are highly recommended. Sing fewer songs. Reduce the number of verses. Be mindful of how long a song goes.

Another consideration that must be made where music is concerned is that of how we adapt displaying song lyrics in the online experience. Many churches project song lyrics on screens during in-person worship so that parishioners can sing along. A common practice in physical gatherings of worship is to project those lyrics full-screen in the room. When it comes to online, we can't take that same feed and push it to the stream like we would in our physical space. In the room, we have peripheral vision and the ability to see both the leaders and the lyrics simultaneously. Online, if we display what typically goes to the screen, just lyrics and backgrounds, and we do multiple songs, it can be a very long time before we see a human being on screen. The entire portal into the experience of worship online is the screen.

Regardless of what kind of music you do, the presence of the leader on camera is critically important to inviting participation. The lyrics don't lead themselves. The leader leads the lyrics. If you're not already doing so, find a way to get both the lyrics and the leader on screen at the same time.

When full-screen lyrics are up for too long, the voices become disembodied. Depending on when you tune in, if the lyrics are displayed without camera shots mixed in, an online worshiper may have no idea what the singers look like or who is singing.

Getting both the lyrics and the leaders on the screen at the same time can be as simple as having the leader positioned in front of a screen that a camera is capturing and broadcasting, or it can be more complicated, involving third party software with the ability to lay lyrics over the camera shots. I'm sure there is a wide range of tech-savvy and know-how represented in the readers of this book. The range likely spans from those streaming from a smartphone to those using a multi-camera setup with fancy software. Whatever technology you're using, remember to bring the human element to the experience.

Liturgy and Sacraments

In more traditional/liturgical settings, it's important to adapt the practices around sacraments and other participatory elements. Without adaptation, things like communion, baptism, and responsive readings don't often translate one-to-one to the at-home experience. Responsive readings, calls to worship, and prayers benefit greatly from having a digital worship order offered as a downloadable file.

If you do some kind of print piece – a bulletin, worship folder, program, or whatever you may call it in your church – consider also saving a PDF file to include in your chat or video description. You might also include a QR code on screen that will auto-launch a digital file on a phone or tablet. Life.Church's free Church Online Platform (churchonlineplatform.com) allows you to incorporate notes, outlines, links, and more. This creates a more interactive and participatory experience.

Some worshipers may be watching on a smart TV or a device that doesn't show chat. Chat can greatly enhance the experience of worship, making people not in the building feel more a part of worship. Chat allows for prayers to be lifted, reflections to be shared, and questions to be asked. You might consider verbally inviting participants to open up the chat on a second device so they can follow along and participate in the conversation taking place throughout worship in real time. I call this "the dual screen experience."

Including a digital worship order allows for the kind of participation that people are accustomed to in in-person worship. Be sure to post this digital worship order along with your archived worship experience so people can participate when they watch on delay too. In addition to having a downloadable worship order, make use of the screen for responsive prayers, calls to worship, and other spoken pieces. For many readers, this is a no-brainer. For others, it may be a new consideration. People at home cannot participate if you don't provide them with the text to do so. Using lower third graphics – that's the technical term for the graphics that come up at the bottom of the screen on television programs – invites interaction from those worshiping online. There's a free app called OBS (Open Broadcast Software, www.obsproject.com) that can help you accomplish this. Paid apps such as Vmix, Wirecast, and Ecamm Live all do the same thing with more features and better support.

Giving

Giving is a very important aspect act of worship. Adaptation is required here as well. With online worship, it's impossible to physically pass the plate to regular attenders and guests who may be gathered from any number of geographical locales. Thankfully, years before Covid-19 arrived, digital giving platforms sprang up to make giving easier than ever before.

For many years I've encouraged churches to embrace digital or online giving in my consultation work. Pre-Covid, many resisted this technology saying things like, "We don't want to have to pay fees on our offering. We'll lose part of those gifts if we use a processing service for giving." While it is true that there are fees associated with some of these services, most of them will allow the giver to cover the fees. Let me also point out that you lose 100% of the gifts people can't give, because they're not in person.

If we want young people to participate in a life of stewardship in our churches, we must steer clear of expecting them to write a check or send in cash. They're much more likely to Cashapp, Venmo, or PayPal you an offering than they are to break out the pen and physical checkbook.

Online giving opens up new possibilities for parishioners and I've heard numerous churches who had embraced online giving say that their giving did not drop but stayed steady and even increased during the pandemic.

There are two basic aspects of giving we should consider as it pertains to Both/And worship. First is that we need to teach people how to give. Just as many had to learn to use Zoom, YouTube, and Facebook in 2020, learning how to give online takes some handholding for certain segments of a congregation.

If you don't already have one, create a tutorial video. It can be fancy, or very simple. Walk them through the process step-by-step. Show them how to use your app, website, or whatever service you use. You might periodically show this video in your worship, both online and in-person, but you can also post a link to it in your chat and verbally reference it when you're inviting people to give. Don't forget to mention all of the ways worshipers can give, from snail mail to the offering plate, and digitally as well.

The second aspect of giving to emphasize in your church is telling people why to give. "Why" is as important if not more important than "how." Are you telling the stories of where your offerings are going? You should be.

In the late 90s, I got my start in ministry at a large church near Dayton, Ohio, called Ginghamsburg United Methodist Church. During my years on staff there, and in the years that followed, I remember hearing my friend and mentor, lead pastor Mike Slaughter say, "Money follows mission, not church budgets." Let that sink in. People don't get excited about paying the utility bill. They do however get excited about being part of a movement that is making a real difference in people's lives.

Prior to my arrival on staff there, my colleague Len Wilson, who was the media minister, developed a style of video called a "Mission Moment." The idea behind these two-to-three-minute videos was to highlight the ministry of the church, showing parishioners all of the ways they were making a difference through giving. In a very short period of time, the staff recognized a pattern had developed in response to these videos. When a Mission Moment was shown prior to the offering being taken, the offering would go up. People would be more inspired than might be typical after seeing the mission of the church featured in these short snapshots.

Highlight what you're doing to make a difference in your community and in the world. Show a video. Share some photos. Interview someone involved with a project you're supporting. Just tell your story! You don't have to have a professional editor or photographer. It can be simple. We all carry around production studios in our pockets now. Pull out those phones and hit record. Be intentional about capturing what your church is doing to minister to your community.

Telling these missional stories does inspire action. In the spring of 2021, I began coaching Spry Church in York, Pennsylvania. Pastor Ken Loyer and his team have a strong desire to lean into creating a Both/And worship experience and wanted some guidance on how to do that. In our monthly coaching sessions, we had regular conversations about the importance of telling the story of why giving was important along with an invitation on how to give. Several months into our work together, Ken wrote to tell me about an encouraging letter he'd receive that made it clear their efforts were making a difference.

One afternoon he opened the mail to find a hand-written note from one of his parishioners expressing how meaningful a recent stewardship series had been. She shared that while she'd only experienced it online, she found it to be one of the most inspiring messages she'd ever heard on the topic of stewardship. Accompanying the very heartfelt letter was a sizable check along with a sincere thank you. All of this occurred without her ever stepping foot into the building.

Give them an ROI

The final adaptation I'd like to invite you to consider is to stop beginning your worship experience with the least compelling thing you have to offer – the announcements. Instead, give worshipers both online and in-person an ROI. ROI in the business world stands for "return on investment." What will people get if they invest their time with you? Answer that right up front. Give people online a reason to stay. Tell them what's coming. Share a rundown of what's to come rather than starting with a bunch of boring information.

One common way we start worship often goes like this: An opening song is played, and then someone steps to the mic and says:

> Good morning, welcome to worship, we're so glad you're here. Let me tell you about what's happening in the life of our church." Followed by several boring and very disconnected announcements, the host might continue with words like, "First, our women's group is meeting on Zoom on Monday night at 6:00 PM. If you're a woman in our church, we hope you'll sign up to participate. Next, some of our youth will be heading to summer camp this summer. We're conducting a bake sale to raise money

> to help them cover the costs. If you're a baker, be sure to bring something in next week..." ARE YOU BORED YET? I am and I wrote these announcements.

Instead of starting with the least compelling thing you have to offer, hook them right off the bat with an ROI. It might go something like this:

> Hello and welcome to worship, my name is Jason and I serve on the worship team here at Acme church. We're glad you're here. We're in the middle of a series entitled 'Finding Your Faith in a Season of Fear.' In week one we talked about what fear is and why we feel it. In week two we talked about facing our fear through scripture. Today we're talking about praying through our fear. We're so glad you'll be joining us. Over the next 40 minutes, we'll worship together in song, pray together, hear some inspiring scripture, and you'll experience a message of hope that will help you face whatever fears you may be dealing with in your life right now. We invite you to lean in and fully participate. Let's worship the God who is with us in all that we face!" And then you might go into a time of singing, prayer, scripture, sermon, and anything else that you might regularly do.

Now, let me boldly suggest a major change - if it is your practice to do announcements at the beginning of worship, STOP DOING ANNOUNCEMENTS. That's right. Stop doing announcements. Instead, move that info to the end, and reimagine it in the form of action steps. Craft the language so that info fits your topic of the day. When you do this, those opportunities begin to feel like an extension of the sermon, and they give people something to do next. They feel like they have purpose.

Here's what that might look like. After the sermon, as the last thing you do, you might do something like this (and this could be the pastor, or it could be a layperson):

> I hope over the last 40 minutes you've found what you needed to face the fears that are before you. Friends, we're a church that actively finds our faith in many ways. I want to give you three opportunities to live into what we've been talking about today. First, our women's group is meeting online on Monday night. I can't think of a better way to face our fears and build our faith than to do so in relationship with others. I hope if you're a woman in our church you'll participate in this uplifting gathering. Second, we have some young people in this church who are hoping to go to summer camp in July. Camp is a great place to find and strengthen faith. Junior high and high school represent a season of life that involves a decent amount of fear. From school pressure to peer pressure, Covid con-

> cerns, and more, our young people are in the thick of it. To send our kids to camp, we're going to have a bake sale fundraiser. All of the proceeds will go to raise money to pay for camp for our kids."

Do you see what I did there? These are no longer announcements, they're action steps that feel intentional and are rooted in the big idea of the day. Stop starting with announcements (something very easy to turn off), and start doing action steps (something that establishes what's next). Announcements don't have to be a burden to the flow of your service, they can be an opportunity to live into the fullness of one's faith.

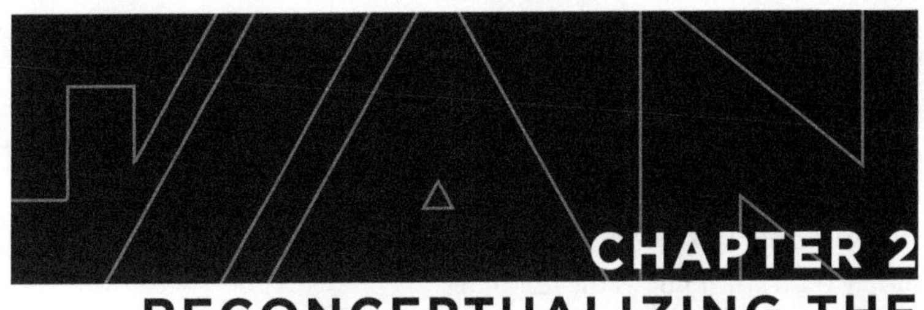

CHAPTER 2 RECONCEPTUALIZING THE ONLINE EXPERIENCE

"I'm not crazy about reality, but it's still the only place to get a decent meal."

– Groucho Marx

The last rollercoaster I rode was the tallest, fastest, and most death-defying coaster I'd ever been on. It was also the one I felt the least amount of reaction to. In fact, I didn't feel anything at all when I rode it. No butterflies. No g-forces. No wind in my face. Nothing.

The only item on my 2020 Christmas list was the Oculus Quest 2 virtual reality headset. My wife was nice enough to tip off Saint Nick, and I found one under the tree on Christmas morning. A day or two following the unboxing, I "rode" a virtual coaster with my dad. He was 30 miles away, sitting in his living room with his own Quest headset strapped to his face.

The experience of riding a rollercoaster in VR is similar in some ways to riding the real thing. It starts with the familiar click-click-click sound in rapid succession as you climb the lift hill to the top. While ascending the hill, you can peer over the sides of your car at the somewhat convincingly rendered terra firma below. The ambience of birds chirping, a breeze blowing, and the rustling of trees can be heard in the distance, as you talk to the person sitting next to you in the car (all in perfectly rendered stereo sound).

What's not the same is the nervous energy you might feel as you ride to the top. You're not tempted to hold your breath or clinch the lap bar in front of you. You don't catch air, or strain to keep your head from banging against the restraints. And while it looks cool, it feels nothing like riding an actual coaster. There was one thing that was absolutely real about this experience: the sense of connection I had sitting next to the avatar version of my dad who was boisterously laughing his head off down every hill and around every corner. But the coaster itself was a disappointment. While it was a relatively close approximation of what it feels like to ride a rollercoaster, it simply wasn't the same as the real thing.

One of my least favorite terms for online worship is "virtual worship." Virtual experiences are not actual experiences. Worship that is experienced online isn't a pretend version of worship. When done in such a way that it is reimagined for an audience not physically gathered, it can be a true experience of worship for those participating in the digital space. In the same way I felt a real connection with my dad on the VR coaster, we can build meaningful interaction into the experience where those participating will feel a part of it. There's nothing virtual about that. It's actual worship. But are we building real connections with people online?

My friend Anne Bosarge, pastor of The Chapel Online, says, "We have to recognize the difference between content and connection. The church and worship of the past was largely about receiving content. Now it's all about connection. We can create connection both in-person and online."

Anne knows a lot about making real connections. She's leading a congregation that meets online exclusively. Birthed in March of 2020, this faith community has members from 24 countries, and it's growing like wildfire.

Reimagining how we craft worship - taking it from book to film – is only half the battle. We must also consider reimagining the experience of worship.

ITERATE AND INNOVATE

Perhaps the most exciting thing about worship in 2020 for me was seeing all of the experimentation happening from week to week in online worship. Churches who had never before hit (or heard of) the "go live" button on a streaming platform gave it a try for the first time. What happened from there was at times incredibly inspiring and other times painfully abysmal. Sometimes it was moving and on other occasions comical – and not on purpose. Here are a few recreations of some of the things I witnessed in March and April of 2020:

I call this first one "The Cheap Seats." Slap a camera in the back of the room and go about business as usual. Problem is, if you tune in and you don't know any of these people, you have no idea who is actually leading. This method of shooting worship requires parishioners to use a magnifying glass to see anything or anyone.

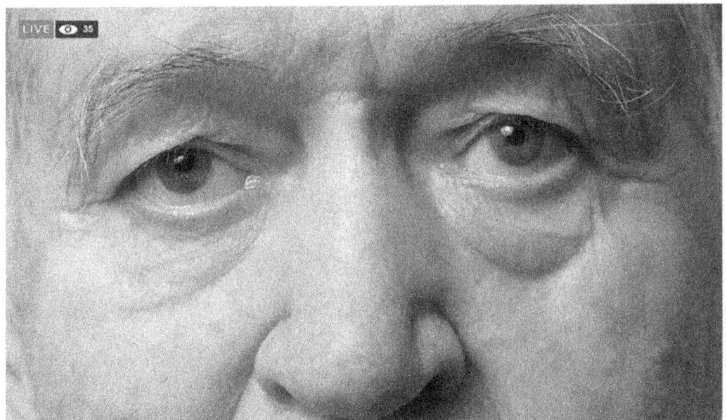

I call this next one "Too Close for Comfort." While I am a fan of close-ups over ultra-wide shots, this is taking things a bit too far. These folks might want to back the camera up a hair. And speaking of hair, this poor guy might want to trim his eyebrow hairs before the next stream.

Next up, we have what I call "Surveillance Camera Worship." This one is great because it has night vision, and no one steals anything off the altar table anymore.

I lovingly refer to this one as "Defying Gravity." This church's tagline is "Come hang out with us." There's a lot about online worship that feels a bit upside down, but this is taking it to the extreme.

Here we have what I call, "The Ninety-Degree Angle." Sometimes our worship goes a little sideways, and here's the proof. Early on, I saw this kind of thing on Facebook quite often.

We'll take the Gospel to people who need it using any means possible. I call this next one "Ring doorbell worship." Just step out on your front porch and broadcast the Good News to anyone who can receive it. Or maybe it's just for whomever is watching your security feed.

And finally, I am a big fan of this last one. I call it "Zoom Filtered Worship." You may find yourself telling people you are not a cat during worship, like happened in what is probably the most famous Zoom meme video ever featuring a call from the 394th Judicial District Court of Texas. A lawyer's daughter had been playing on his computer prior to his court appearance and the filter had been left on. Despite his best attempts, he could not figure out how to turn it off and hilarity ensued.

You can view the video here:
www.youtube.com/watch?v=TDNP-SWgn2w

From Groove to Rut

In time, weekly iterations that created a sense of intrigue, mystery, and excitement – that really made people want to tune in – gave way to a more templated approach in many churches. As the weeks went on, worship planners found two or three tricks that worked, and they started using them over and over. The problem with a trick that is done over and over is that, in time with repetition, a trick is no longer a trick. It becomes predictable and loses its luster.

After increasing online attendance brought on by the shelter-in-place orders stabilized, an interesting phenomenon occurred that many struggled to understand. On Mother's Day weekend 2020, just months after many went online for the first time, numerous churches reported a significant attendance drop. My Facebook feed was filled with post after post from churches of every size and style, all lamenting the drop. What made it even more of a head-scratcher was the fact that Mother's Day is traditionally one of the best attended Sundays of the year. As I began to ponder why this happened, a theory began to emerge. I believe Mother's Day 2020 was an attendance bomb for two reasons.

First, we were still in lockdown. While sons and daughters will typically tag along with mom to church on her special day, churches were still closed in May, making that tradition impossible. Mother's Day came early enough in the pandemic that families had been isolating and avoiding in-person contact with one another. This might have been the one occasion that families broke the shelter-in-place protocols to go celebrate mom together, even if it meant visiting outdoors without physical contact. That choice may have resulted in families skipping the stream for some desperately needed in-person time.

The second reason - and the one I believe was a major contributing factor to this drop - is that enough time had passed from March to May that churches were no longer experimenting in the same way that they had in the early months of the pandemic. The novelty was beginning to wear off, and worship started to become much more predictable. It may also have been that fatigue had set in. We were tired of screens and needed a break. Mother's Day was a great excuse not to tune in one week. What happened next however leads me to believe that wasn't the main reason.

During this period, I was hosting and participating in weekly Monday morning Zoom calls organized around learning from what was happening the Sunday before in online worship. Basically, we were Monday morning quarterbacking it. A common shared experience indicated that many churches took several weeks to get people back to the pre-Mother's Day numbers. In other words, the drop didn't immediately bounce back the following week. Some of the excitement was gone, and I blame predictability for the decreasing numbers. Whatever the case may be, the innovative and malleable spirit that existed in the early months of the pandemic started to dry up as the social distancing continued long beyond when any of us expected it to. Truth is, it was easier to do the same thing every week than it was to continue to innovate and keep the experimentation going.

Worship started to return to the pre-pandemic templates of the past. People more-or-less knew what they'd miss if they tuned in late, and some just started missing worship all together. Others discovered what TiVo and

DVR taught us decades ago: if you watch on delay, you can fast forward past the pieces that don't interest you. Ouch! I know that is hard to hear, but it's true. Some of what we include in worship is being skipped on demand and on delay.

Now, I do recognize that we're people of ritual and tradition. There is some comfort and even meaning derived from engaging in some of the same things each week. For some it's like a warm fuzzy security blanket to know the order of worship by heart. However, without iteration and innovation, our worship starts to be become a bit "spoiler-ish."

And nobody likes a spoiler.

> The *Oxford English Dictionary* (via Google) defines a spoiler as: a description of an important plot development in a television show, movie, or book which if previously known may reduce surprise or suspense for a first-time viewer or reader.

When our patterns become overly predictable from week-to-week, newcomers may begin to perceive worship as a bit rote without much of a sense of intrigue about what's to come. For example, if the first week someone attends worship online the order includes three songs, a welcome, a prayer, a scripture reading, and a sermon - all in that order - and the following week it's exactly the same thing again, and the week following it's the same again, it's not hard to spot the pattern. Worship becomes spoiled. It might look like this:

> Week one's order: 3 songs, a welcome, a prayer, a scripture reading, and a sermon.
>
> SPOILER ALERT – week two's order: 3 songs, a welcome, a prayer, a scripture reading, and a sermon.
>
> SPOILER ALERT – week three's order: 3 songs, a welcome, a prayer, a scripture reading, and a sermon.

And over and over and over. The excitement of the early weeks of the pandemic was that the order was always evolving. Part of the fun of joining each week was seeing what was going to happen. And then, relatively quickly, we standardized it.

I live and work near Dayton, Ohio. The Iams pet food company was originally founded in a small feed mill not far from Dayton back in 1946. While Paul Iams was its founder, it was Clay Mathile who took Iams from a local unknown company making $100,000 a year in revenue, to a $900 million a year household name. Clay is an innovator who pushed the company to keep trying new things, first buying half the company and eventually buying the entire operation. He eventually created an organization of such great value, Procter & Gamble bought him out.[1]

Not far from where I live sits a business center also founded by Mathile. Aileron (named after the mechanical component on airplanes used to provide lateral balance) is an organization designed to empower businesses large and small to thrive and grow. For several years I had a membership to their campus and would visit there often. On one of the walls hangs one of my favorite quotes of all time. Clay says: "The only difference between a rut and a groove is how long you've been in it." I love using this metaphor for considering cycles of innovation and stagnation. In March of 2020, the church found a new groove both collectively and individually. It was equal parts terrifying and inspiring. It moved the needle. People began paying attention, and churches extended their reach. In time that groove became a rut, and we started repeating ourselves, because there was just less effort involved in doing the two or three things we'd figured out. Some allowed worship to go on autopilot, and less and less intentionality was applied to the online experience. A rut eventually becomes so deep it takes quite a bit of energy to get up and over the edges to start a new groove.

If it's been a while since you've tried something new, I'd invite you to remember those early days of the pandemic and how exciting it was. Remember the way your congregation was cheering you on. Remember the exhilaration you felt experimenting with the format and tools. Think back on the response you received from your people and those whom maybe you didn't yet know. Sure, it wasn't all sunshine and rainbows, but if you're at all like the tens of thousands of people I've had the privilege of speaking to this past year, you were reaching more people than ever.

Am I saying that you have to have a completely different order every week? No, not at all. I'm not suggesting you create an unsustainable routine of breaking the mold every week. You'll completely wear yourself out. I am

1. "Iams," Wikipedia, accessed September 23, 2021, https://en.wikipedia.org/wiki/Iams.

however suggesting that changing things up from time to time keeps people excited about coming to worship both in-person and online. Without spoilers, worshipers have a sense of intrigue and excitement.

When I was on staff at Ginghamsburg Church in the late '90s, we tried constantly to experiment with the order of worship. It was just in our DNA. A member of the church once told me that he never wanted to be late or miss a service for fear that he'd miss something incredible. That kind of intrigue doesn't happen when worship is completely predictable. We did sometimes go a bit overboard at Ginghamsburg, striving to never or very rarely repeat ourselves. That kind of overkill leads to burnout. You shouldn't feel the pressure to always top yourself. It's an unwinnable battle. Instead strive to keep it fresh from time to time.

If you preach in a series, you might consider designing a format that each week in the series follows. A pattern for the duration of the series would create familiarity, and then in the next series, you change the template and do something different. Maybe you could include a reflection question for four weeks during a series. Ask a question at the beginning of worship and encourage people to text in, chat in, or write down their responses. For example, ask them to reflect on a single question, "Who is Jesus to you?" Give people time to respond, and then save room in the sermon to read and respond to some of those reflections.

Maybe in the next series you change up the order a bit. Here's a radical idea: start with the message and allow everything that follows (music, prayer, liturgy) to become a reflection of the lessons taught in the message.

Another series could include a tactile moment where you invite people to interact with an object in the physical space, while providing instruction for how to participate from home.

One church I'm presently coaching in North Carolina is developing several templates that can be rotated through series by series. In the same way a television series might end with a cliffhanger that resets the narrative for the next season (motivating people to come back), you too might consider enticing people into the next format and series with some different elements.

Another congregation I'm working with in East Ohio, led by Pastor Kimberly Arbaugh (Carrollton First United Methodist Church), is reimagining altogether what online worship can be. She and her team are creating a multi-week series that will air on YouTube for a purely online audience.

Together with her team, we brainstormed a tweak to the naming convention of this new online expression. Rather than calling them "sermon series," she's calling them "seasons," and each week is considered "an episode." They'll shoot somewhere in the neighborhood of six to eight episodes per season and will premiere them once a week until they hit the end of the run. They'll then work on the next season, which will ideally air a few weeks later or whenever the new episodes are ready. This eases the burden of having to crank something out every week, allows them to bunch production up, and affords them the design of a format for each season. The current plan has them changing up the format each time, along with the topic, setting, and so on. This fresh approach should keep people coming back for more, as it'll be both familiar and different each time.

As I write, they're in development of this new faith expression and hoping to launch it in the fall of 2021. The working title (which I love) is "The Experience." It's a totally new way of thinking about church online that will be friendly to both those in church and those with no church experience whatsoever.

Iterate Forwards, Don't Revert Backwards

At the same time that we were panicking about our church buildings being off limits to us, late night television was struggling with what to do sans studios, audiences, equipment, and crews. Show hosts found themselves wrestling with the same predicament we were experiencing. As they say in the entertainment industry, "the show must go on," and it didn't take long for adjustments to be made to the format. It was both fascinating and educational to watch how comedians such as Jimmy Fallon and Stephen Colbert tackled this new reality.

In my Both/And webinar, I wanted to help leaders recognize the value of iteration. I suspected it wouldn't be long for churches to go backwards rather than forwards when they re-entered their buildings, so I wanted to give them a picture of what iteration looked like. To show the iterative progression that *The Tonight Show with Jimmy Fallon* went through from pre-pandemic to when Jimmy returned to the studio, I put together three short video excerpts.

The first clip was the typical pre-pandemic *Tonight Show* opening. The clip begins with frenetic camera movements, lights, graphics, and The Roots

(Jimmy's band) pounding out their high energy theme song. Cameras fly over the audience as the curtain opens and Jimmy jumps out with a snazzy three-piece suit on, ready to deliver the monologue. Audience members sit elbow-to-elbow, row after row after row. This is the way things were long before the words "social distancing" were spoken ad nauseam on the nightly news.

Next, I show a clip from the "at home" edition of *The Tonight Show*. On this segment entitled "Thank You Cards," Jimmy's two young daughters are assisting on camera. They're all inside a giant camping tent. The whole family is sitting on sleeping bags, pillows, and a giant stuffed snowman. Seated to Jimmy's right is his eldest daughter. She's holding a handful of images printed on 8.5 x 11 sheets of paper. These stand in for what would typically be onscreen graphics. She is to lift them up in time with Jimmy's scripted jokes. To his left is his younger daughter. She struggles to stay on task the entire time. Her job is to cue the familiar piano-based "Thank You Card" music by pressing play on the iPad sitting in front of her. Behind the camera is Fallon's wife. For all we know she's filming on a smartphone. She does an admirable job of framing the shot, but it's tough, because she is giggling as she watches her family struggle to finish the bit. You can hear every disembodied chuckle as the sketch progresses.

As Jimmy struggles to read jokes off the iPhone he has clutched in his hands, his daughters do their best to keep up with their respective roles. He can barely get through the material, because his daughters aren't performing their tasks with much success. At one point, mid-way through a joke, his younger daughter goes to the window of the tent and says, "I'm going to go look and see where doggie is." He stops and says, "No, you've gotta come back and press the button." She continues to peer out the window scanning for the dog. After he coaxes her back to the iPad, she hits the play button multiple times in a row, and he can barely contain his laughter. In fact, he doesn't contain it at all. He makes two or three attempts to finish the joke, says "sorry" multiple times, and then finally reaches the punchline. As this clip plays, the chat lights up with numerous "LOLs" and "hahahas." Many other comments scroll across the chat window indicating that participants are enjoying the segment. The whole thing is quite charming. Let's be honest, production-wise, it's a total mess. The sound isn't great, the camera work is all over, and the talent can't get through the material. Despite all of that, it was a beautiful iteration of the previous incarnation of the show. In my opinion, it is some of the most compelling stuff Jimmy has ever done.

Was it perfect? No. Was it authentic? Absolutely. Let's not forget that this was being broadcast to an international audience. If that iteration of *The Tonight Show* was acceptable (and it was), everything we've been doing online since March 2020 has been too. Every church leader involved in the execution of online worship should breathe a little easier after experiencing such an iteration.

Jimmy's iteration should allow us to take a big deep breath. I'm going to invite you right now as you hold this book in your hand to inhale a big deep breath though your nose. Now exhale out through your mouth. Breathe easy. Like Fallon at home, what you've been doing this last year has been so important, and you're doing just fine.

My favorite thing about showing the *Tonight Show* piece is that it helps churches understand that authenticity is more important than being slick or perfect. What you do in front of the camera is more important than which camera you use. How you re-imagine the story and tell it matters more than if you're shooting with a smartphone streaming directly to YouTube, or if you have three cameras and fancy switching software streaming to multiple sources. Let's focus on showing people Jesus in an authentic way, and let the Spirit do the rest. When we remember in the forefront of our minds that there are people on the other side of the camera, just as Fallon did, we can create compelling moments that people will be drawn to.

The last clip I show from *The Tonight Show* is from the week Jimmy first returned to the studio after lockdown. I ask webinar attendees to make observations about the clip as it's playing. It's always fun to see what they share.

The clip begins right from the opening music, which is significantly different from the previous iteration of the show. The new music cue has a lazy jazz feel to it that is playful and mellow. The first shot in the sequence features Jimmy walking down the stairs of what appears to be an apartment. When he gets to the bottom, he takes a mask out of his pocket and secures it over his nose and mouth. In his hand is a briefcase and a sport coat.

In the next shot he leaps over a construction barrier as he makes his way through the streets of New York. Observant webinar participants always point out the symbolism of jumping over those barriers, which represent the hurdles we were all facing during this pandemic. The sequence continues with a leisurely stroll through the streets of the Big Apple. The camera cuts to a shot of 30 Rockefeller Center, and we hear the announcer utter the same words he's spoken at the beginning of every show since Jimmy took over hosting duties. There's now a noticeable chilled vibe in the announcer's voice.

The next shots take us into the studio where crew members roll away chairs from the floor level of the studio. All of the other seats are all covered, indicating they are not in use. The sequence cuts to shots of the band who are noticeably separated into two levels - half on a second-floor platform, the other half at floor level. A pan across the stage reveals a brand-new set that looks more like a fancy New York City apartment than a studio theater with a curtain, desk, and couch for guests to sit on.

Jimmy saunters out to the stage with no fanfare. He's wearing sneakers, black jeans, a long sleeve white t-shirt, and a sport coat over top of it. He sits on a stool and turns to talk directly to the camera.

Webinar attendees point out that it's a much more subdued vibe. They appreciate that this new format acknowledges what the world is going through. It feels more casual, more personal, and more real. Even the set reflects the fact that – at the time it was airing – we were mostly all at home more so than out in theaters.

As the observations continue to cascade down the chat window, I will often stop and ask the rhetorical question, "Jason, why are we watching *The Tonight Show*? What does this have to do with church?" I'm quick to follow that up by pointing out that these three iterations are something that every person involved in the dreaming, development, and deployment of worship can learn from.

Surely the temptation was there for Jimmy and his producers to go right back to where the show was prior to the pandemic. There must have been some consideration and conversation about firing back up the lights, readying the curtain, pressing the suit and tie, and getting back to the format they'd done for years. But that's not what they chose to do. Very wisely, they considered that we'd all been locked down for almost a year, and to go back to where things were prior to all of this with no transition - after watching Jimmy from home for so long - would feel out of touch. It would be jarring.

Just as *The Tonight Show* staff made the call to iterate forward, we too should do the same. The temptation many leaders face is to go backward.

"Let's just return to the way it was." "Let's pretend like none of this happened." Churches who make this choice may erase all of the forward momentum gained when Covid-19 forced us into the 21st century.

My friend Pastor Mike Slaughter is famous for saying, "If you put it up for a vote, the people will always vote to go back to Egypt." So true! Many are not willing to go through the desert of discomfort that change brings about and instead want to retreat to what is safe, familiar, and comfortable. Friends, we're much of the way through the desert. If we'll just press on a little longer and lean in a bit more, we can make some permanent changes that will allow us to reach more people for Christ than ever before. We can't go back!

The pandemic happened. We can't pretend we didn't all live through it. In the same way my wife can no longer walk me all the way to the gate and watch me walk down the jet bridge when flying post-9/11, we must also consider that the way we engage in worship has forever changed as a result of Covid-19. We have to resist the temptation to go backwards. We must iterate forwards and find new ways to express the gospel in light of all we've learned during the pandemic.

By the time you read this book, unless there's a resurgence, you are already back in the building. Let me point out that the building represents safety and comfort. It's been a while since you were living in the thick of a lockdown or limited in-person gatherings. Reflect back on the ways you had to re-think ministry when it was unavailable to us.

The great blogger, author, and thought leader Carey Nieuwhof had a word of warning to share with leaders during the period where we were shut down. He says, "Too many church leaders will step right back into the past the moment they step back in their building."[2] As you examine your worship experience, have you stepped into the past or have you leaped forward into the new strategy that considers the Both/And crowd? We must iterate forward and not revert backward.

Both/And Think Tank

To ensure that you do not go backwards and instead find the next iteration of worship at your church, I'd encourage you to start a Both/And

2. Carey Nieuwhof, "Avoid This Big Mistake: Stepping Back into the Past When You Step Back into Your Building," Careynieuwhof.com, https://careynieuwhof.com/avoid-this-big-mistake-stepping-back-into-the-past-when-you-step-back-into-your-building/.

think tank. This group should be made up of leaders who represent people who primarily worship in person and those who primarily worship online respectively. The group should look carefully and methodically at the worship experience that was offered prior to the pandemic in-person (and even online, if you were streaming then). Systematically discuss each aspect of worship, from music, to liturgy, media, preaching, guest welcome, streaming, and anything else that was a part of the weekly routine. Ask which pieces resonated then, and which pieces still resonate today, taking into consideration an audience that is partially in-person and partially online. Boldly consider which aspects of worship no longer work post-pandemic both in-person and online. Remember that people spent a year in their pajamas with the ability to worship with coffee in their hands. They probably experienced a greatly reduced worship experience length-wise too. They had the ability to skip past parts of worship. How should that shape the next iteration of worship? Be organized and take good notes throughout this process. Try to be as detached as possible when offering feedback. Find a good scribe who can record the notes without prejudice.

Next, take the same look at the worship you offered online during the pandemic - especially during the period when no one was in your building. Some of the practices that worked great with an audience completely online may have continued but now don't work as well with a hybrid audience. What aspects of your online worship that historically worked well then don't work today? And what things still carry over? Ask how every aspect of worship you plan can include both people gathered physically, and those who are gathered digitally.

Your Both/And think tank should also review your worship together as a group. Pull it up on a screen and collectively experience it together. No fast forwarding allowed! We're often so tied up in the planning and deployment of worship that we never actually experience it. This is your chance to see what it's like to worship at your church online. Where do you feel engaged? Where do you feel disconnected? How can you create moments that lean into the former and avoid the latter?

In the same way that *The Tonight Show's* third iteration didn't look like the previous two, the next iteration of your worship shouldn't look exactly like your pre-pandemic worship, or your pandemic-era worship. When you consider a Both/And crowd, you must find a happy medium. Most of us did not have time to build an intentional hybrid strategy when we began.

Now's your chance. I am not suggesting that you throw everything out and start over from scratch. An iteration by its very nature is based on what's come before. Your previous two iterations will inform your new one. If you simply choose one of the previous two, you'll very likely create more of an EITHER/OR scenario.

Who should you recruit for this team?

- Advocates for both experiences
- People willing to support any potential outcome (even if they don't like it)
- Those who can put their ego aside
- Leaders who can remain unmarried to their ideas
- Out-of-the-box thinkers
- A combo of church veterans and newcomers
- People who have worshiped online exclusively (if applicable)
- An unbiased facilitator or scribe

While every team I've worked with is a little different, these are the steps I generally take when leading a think tank:

1) START WITH THE "WHY?"

Think tank conversations work best when they are rooted in a shared vision. Start first with why you're redesigning your worship experience for Both/And in the first place. I personally like to root the process in a biblical story and use it as a guide for multiple conversations.

2) BUILD RELATIONSHIPS

It's hard to do creative work when you don't know each other, especially when the topic is heavy, like changing worship methodologies. Gather around a meal; do something to build relationships within the team. The best teams start not just with the work of the team, but the work among the team.

3) HAVE FUN

The best part of being a part of a think tank is that it can be a lot of fun. Keep it light and loose. Brainstorming can be an absolute blast. Bring creative things into the space. Play-doh, Legos, fidget toys, and the like give people a creative way to channel their energy. A think tank shouldn't be stressful; focus on making it fun.

4) HAVE A PROCESS

While brainstorming can be fun when there's freedom to go in any direction, guardrails help you stay on the road and avoid driving off a cliff. Establish a process up front to help you funnel your creativity toward consensus. Encourage everyone to participate, and maybe even build in a moment for each person to share their thoughts in a systematic way. Do your brainstorming together in the group rather than in isolation where people report back their individual ideas. That often leads to creative roadblocks, because people become overly invested in their own ideas. Determine from the outset how many times you are going to meet. I recommend at a minimum three meetings, spread out over a period of months.

5) COVENANT TOGETHER

The work of a think tank can be fun, but it can also get stressful. It's imperative for the team to covenant together to participate in the entire process, and when it's done, be a cheerleader for whatever decision is made. One church I led through a think tank process only had two rules for participants:

Rule one: You had to commit to being at all three meetings.

Rule two: you had to be willing to support the decision of the team even if you didn't agree.

If you couldn't do both of those, you couldn't participate in the think tank. Thankfully, some people were honest enough to say they couldn't agree to rule two and they bowed out. I'm sure this saved us a ton of heartache and harsh debate.

6) BRING MUTUAL RESPECT

Egos get in the way in church life, especially when there are educated and skilled people in the room. Team members must bring mutual respect and support for the ideas of others. They must also be willing to let go and stay unmarried to their ideas. I've seen way too many "creative bullies" kill the momentum of a team.

7) KEEP IT FLOWING

The more ideas a team has, the better when it comes to re-imagining worship for a Both/And world. Use a dry erase board or a flip chart and fill it up. No ideas are bad ideas when brainstorming. The last think tank process I led had five distinct ideas for how to carry out its goals before selecting the final one to implement.

8) DETERMINE A GOAL

After you've done all this amazing work to re-imagine what Both/And can look like at your church, how's it going to happen? When's it going to happen? Whose responsibility is it to do what? A lot can be lost from brainstorming to execution, so make sure your last think tank session includes time to determine goals and assign action steps with measurables built in.

Once this work is complete, you'll constantly have to fight the temptation to go backwards. What's behind us feels nostalgic, safe, and comfortable. What's ahead is unknown. Iterating forward can be an exhilarating ride full of possibilities and new movements. Reverting backwards means losing the momentum you've gained in this season.

PREPARE

While I wholeheartedly believe that authenticity is more important than being slick or perfect in our execution of Both/And worship, we do not have a license to just throw it together and hope for the best. We must properly prepare for the worship we deploy both in-person and online.

The argument has been made numerous times in live events and online discussion groups that I've been a part of over the years that pre-planning somehow limits the Holy Spirit's work in the worship. The notion that the Spirit can somehow be less active in the worship we prepare ahead of time is unbelievable to me. I often think about Jesus' temptation in the wilderness when I hear that concern raised. Matthew establishes that Jesus was led into the wilderness by the Spirit to face 40 days of temptation by Satan. Satan tries every which way he can think of to tempt Jesus, offering him everything from power to food when he was hungry. Each of these temptations is met with scripture. Jesus came prepared. Jesus quoted scriptures he undoubtedly learned and studied as a boy and throughout his life in order to counter Satan's onslaught of temptations. The Spirit led Jesus into the wilderness. Jesus didn't call out to the Spirit every time he was challenged saying in the moment, "Hey can you take this one?" No, he did the work ahead of time. He was ready and prepared for anything. The second scripture Jesus quotes to the devil to shut him down comes from Deuteronomy 6:16. It reads, "Do not put the Lord your God to the test." Sometimes I feel like leaders who make excuses for not planning ahead and properly preparing for worship should re-read this verse. Why put the Lord our God to the test by not working out the plan ahead of time?

A number of years ago, I was speaking at the largest United Methodist Church in the USA, Church of the Resurrection, at their Leadership Institute. During one session I sat in on, lead pastor Adam Hamilton was asked if all of the pre-planning they did limited the Spirit. With only seconds to formulate a response, I could tell he'd been asked this question before and had an answer already prepared in his mental database. I loved his response. He said, "Do you really think the Spirit doesn't know what's going to happen on the day you're planning for, the day you're planning it?" In other words, our omniscient God isn't bound by our timeline. The Spirit is present yesterday, today, and tomorrow all at the same time. The Spirit can be just as present in the planning of a future worship experience, knowing what's going to happen, as the Spirit can be on the day you're deploying that worship. The Spirit can move at any time.

When our audience expanded in 2020 due to the addition or reimagining of online worship, we garnered the attention of a whole lot of newcomers. A lot of people with little to no church history happened upon our services of worship, because we took that worship to social media. What we all must face now is that those people – our guests – don't love us yet. They judge us much more harshly than the people who already love us. Our people love us. They tune in with much less critique and in many cases much lower standards. They don't care that Sister Mildred cannot carry a tune yet is singing a solo on camera for all the world to see. They may have the "bless her heart" mentality in the back of their minds, but a visitor has a "where's the button to close this window" mentality as they are watching. Think about it. We will sit through almost anything when we love people involved in a production.

A few years back, my daughter decided she wanted to play the trumpet in the middle school concert band. We acquired a trumpet, and she went to town practicing her music daily. It sounded like I had a wounded elephant living in my home for weeks. On the night of her first performance, my wife and I sat in the front row with our cameras out ready to record her big moment. Seated next to us on either side were her grandparents, equally excited to support their granddaughter. I hit record to capture the most horrific rendition of "Hot Cross Buns" you'd ever heard. The band played a few scales and then screeched their way through a few other simple tunes. A combination of wincing and fighting off laughter accompanied every performance.

In the small rural school my kids attend, the music directors bunch up the performances, so all of the choirs perform in succession, then each grade's concert band, and so on. After one choir or band finishes all of their numbers, the audience has the option to hang around for the rest of the performances. Or they can bail and go home once their child's group is done. We promptly cleared out when it was time for the next grade to perform as did just about every other family. The thing is, when it was Madeline's turn to perform, we sat there proud of our little girl for the work she'd done to make it this far. We had a connection to her that drove our participation. We love her! Our visitors online do not love us, so when we don't properly prepare or when it's just bad, visitors will tune us out.

Not only do our online visitors not love us, but they are also not committed to us or our worship service and will not think twice about passing us by if we are not addressing them or engaging them.

Talk It, Walk It, Pray It, Do It

In every one of my trainings, I talk about the importance of properly preparing for worship. I stress that it's even more important for online worship than it is for in-person worship. In person, people will sit through almost anything. Congregants will likely not walk out in protest if the sermon is terrible or if the singers can't sing. Online, all a participant has to do is click a button to end whatever agony they're in, and no one will ever know. They are anonymous.

We do not have a captive audience online like we do in the building. If you had the option to do so, you'd very likely click off the middle school concert band performance if your kid wasn't on the stage. So how can we take steps to attempt to make a better experience for those who worship online? I'd suggest doing 4 things each week:

1) TALK IT THROUGH

Without an actual talk-through of your worship order, every member of your team has their own understanding and interpretation of what's to take place in your church. Even if you ask them to read through everything ahead of time, they still have their own interpretations of how things should be carried out. It's important to gather your team in-person, online, or a combo of both to work your way through the order of worship. How are you getting from thing one to thing two? When should this person be in place after that person goes? Are you doing that song the way you've always done it or are you changing things up? Talking through your worship order allows for dialogue, questions to be answered, and sometimes allows you to make tweaks that better the service on the fly. Ask your people to come in (or log in) early to go over the plan. Some will grumble, but in time, this new reality will set in, and hopefully they'll see the value in being better prepared.

2) WALK IT THROUGH

It's wonderful to have a shared understanding of what is supposed to take place in worship, but there's no substitute for actually blocking out and practicing the transitions between the various elements of worship. Transitions have enormous potential to either keep people fully engaged or lose them completely. This is true in-person, but it's greatly magnified online. In the room, because everything is in a person's field of view, a long transition - while distracting - doesn't look like a mistake. If person A finishes the opening spoken piece and then walks off, and person B then stands up and meanders his or her way from the front row to the pulpit, a disconnect can occur. This disconnect in the room is minor, but online it can be a total killer. If an online worshiper turns on the feed and the shot being streamed in that moment is a locked down closeup of the pulpit, and you are between speakers during a long transition, taking twenty seconds for a transition to happen, he or she may just turn the service off and assume it isn't happening.

Many years ago, I read a sobering study that found that in any live event, a bad transition can result in the loss of a fully engaged audience member's attention for up to twenty minutes. If we're following Nona Jones' 25–40-minute guidelines, that's half to nearly all of the service. We simply can't allow that to happen.

Now, I don't think anyone who plans worship thinks of any aspect of worship as "filler," but there are moments that can easily become filler when we're carefree about how we get from one piece to another. When one element ends, and it takes forever for the next to begin, the gap becomes filler. Keeping things tight keeps people engaged. This does not mean that we leave no room for reflection and silence, but there is a dramatic difference between unintended silence and intended silence.

Bad transitions destroy the flow of worship, and without the peripheral vision that comes with being on site, this could lead to the closure of the window and the end of the experience for some viewers. We should always anticipate the next thing about to happen in worship. Leaders should be in place and ready to go when the previous element of worship is concluded. We should never have to watch people walk, turn on mics, look up scripture, or shuffle papers.

3) PRAY IT THROUGH

All of the preparation in the world cannot compare to the power that comes from bathing our worship in prayer. The Holy Spirit is our most important team member, and we should be intentional about inviting the Spirit into our preparatory work. The last thing we want to do is try to do worship in our own power. Circle up your team and invite the Spirit in as a guide and a collaborator. Pray over every aspect of worship from the technology, to the sermon, music, offering, and beyond. Properly preparing involves the one-two punch of understanding, practicing your plan, and the power of the Holy Spirit's presence.

4) DO IT

Once you've done these three things, it's time to do worship. When you've talked it through, walked it through, and prayed it through your plan, doing it becomes much easier. A shared understanding mixed with the muscle memory of running transitions, all backed up with the presence of the Spirit, allows us to create experiences of worship that are transcendent in a Both/And way. Worship may not go exactly the way you thought it might, but all that prep work goes a long way in helping you get back on track if things go off the rails. When everyone knows the plan, has worked it, and has prayed it, minor bumps don't become major train wrecks.

Captive vs. Non-captive Audience

As I write these words, we're about eighteen months into the pandemic. Most weeks I have an average of three to five secret worshiper consultations to conduct each week - mostly for online.

What I became painfully aware of midway through 2020 is that we sometimes take advantage of the fact that we have a captive audience in in-person worship. Frankly, we use the captive audience as a crutch. I know that's a harsh sentiment, but we get away with a multitude of sins in our in-person worship knowing people will not get up and walk out in protest.

If the music isn't properly rehearsed, the sermon goes on too long, there are too many announcements, or if the service is just boring, people in the room are unlikely to get up in the middle and leave.

On the participant side, it's just way too much effort to get up, collect one's things, check kids out of children's church, get in the car and drive across town to another worship experience.

Online, it's only a matter of scrolling down to the next worship service in the feed, or closing a window all together. We do not have a captive audience online. We know this about in-person church, so we can get a little lazy about the prep work. In this Both/And reality, we have to reimagine the experience to give people reason to stay. If we're not careful, we'll give people plenty of reasons to click off.

CREATE A NARRATIVE EXPERIENCE

I've had the honor of consulting with over 250 churches as a secret worshiper over the last decade. I've been to many worship services where it is clear to me that every leader involved in the planning was really only concerned with his or her part of the service and hadn't given much consideration to how that part plays into the entirety of the worship experience. Nothing says siloed worship quite like an experience where the first thing has no relation to the second thing, which has nothing to do with the third thing and, well, you get the point. I've seen this play out too many times to ignore. It looks something like this:

Worship opens with a piece of music. In a more traditional/liturgical setting we might call this the prelude. That is followed by some kind of welcome or spoken word piece. This could be a theme setup or a traditional call to worship. Maybe from there the worship experience moves into a time of singing. The songs could be hymns, camp classics, Taize, or modern music, the style doesn't matter for this example. From there maybe there's a scripture reading, followed by a prayer, and then a children's sermon. That is ultimately followed up by the adult sermon, which is then followed by a closing song.

In this very generic scenario that I've witnessed more times than I can count, there is no narrative tie from element to element. The spoken word never refers to the music, and the music doesn't pick up on any of the ideas captured in the spoken word. The prayer and scripture have no connection to the music or spoken word piece. The children's sermon doesn't reference the scripture for the day, nor does it have anything to do with the adult sermon we're about to experience later in the service. I've even been to worship where the adult sermon has nothing to do with the scripture for the day. Maybe on that Sunday the scripture was read from that week's Revised Common Lectionary text, but the pastor isn't preaching from the Lectionary. In other words, the whole experience is all over the map.

The best way to describe this form of planning - I mean this to be descriptive, not derogatory – is that of a pageant or variety show. Think about it: a pageant is a series of unrelated acts all performed in succession. There are usually no narrative ties. For instance, America's Got Talent is a modern-day pageant/variety show. A typical episode might begin with a singer in the first act, followed by a magician in the second. In the third act there's an acrobat, and the fourth features a ventriloquist. Each and every act can succeed or fail on its own merit, but none of them are tied together by a narrative thread.

The pageant approach to worship provides each leader the opportunity to get up and "do his or her thing" without much regard for the other moments in the service. Rather than building a narrative thread throughout, these disparate moments add up to an experience that is jarring and disjointed. With a captive audience, there's little to no concern for how these moments are received. No one is going to walk out when the children's sermon doesn't relate to the scripture or the adult sermon. Online is a different story. This methodology is confusing – especially to an outsider.

Keep in mind that part of what draws us to the physical worship experience is the community, the sacred space, and the feelings these two give you. Neither of them can be taken advantage of online. For the outsider who doesn't have the warm fuzzies those in the building may have, the lack of narrative may leave them scratching their heads.

Take a mental journey with me for a moment. If you're old enough to remember it, think back to a time when there were just a few channels on television and no DVR or streaming options. I know this sounds like the Dark Ages, and for some readers it has to be completely imagined, because it was never experienced. Hang with me for a moment though.

You turn on the television, and as the cathode-ray tubes warm up, you're greeted onscreen with a new television show you've never seen. Imagine it's your favorite genre. Maybe it's a procedural crime drama, or maybe it's a sitcom. Perhaps it's one of those Hallmark movies, or it could be a sci-fi show. Whatever the case may be, you are completely sucked in from the moment the theme song completes. Only a few minutes in, you're already in love with the cast, setting, and plot. You take note of the day and time, making sure you plan to watch again next week. The first commercial break comes, and you're so enthralled by the first segment of this new show that you don't even get up to grab a snack. You don't want to miss a thing. The break ends, and the show returns, only none of the characters or plot are present from the first segment. Oddly, it's even switched genres. Now it's a police drama, and it started out as a western. For a moment, you wonder if you accidentally turned the channel. Then you remember you're in the Dark Ages, and you literally have to "turn the channel" with a knob, so you know you haven't accidentally done that. You wonder if maybe this is some kind of Twilight Zone type of show where these two disparate stories will eventually come together. You decide to keep watching.

Commercial break number two begins and ends, and the third segment of this show plays the switcheroo on you again. At this point you've just about had it. Nothing is making sense. You've already made a significant time commitment, so you give it one more segment. After another set of commercials ends, the show returns, and it has changed up once again. The final credits run, and you're completely baffled by what you just witnessed. By the time the final credit hits the top of your screen, you've already decided you won't be watching again.

I'd submit to you that for the outsider who is not indoctrinated into our customs, orders, and ritual, this is what non-narrative worship feels like. There's nothing to grab hold of and run with. It's a series of random moments that can be confusing, especially if we don't use language that provides an orientation for the outsider.

I believe a narrative experience is important in-person, but online, I think it's even more critical. Not only does it make things easier to follow, but it makes for a more memorable and actionable experience. It also means that the pastor doesn't have to do all the work in the sermon to get people to where he or she is trying to take them.

Twenty plus years ago when I was on staff at Ginghamsburg UMC, Pastor Mike Slaughter used to joke with our team saying, "It's your job to put me on the one-yard line, so all I have to do is trip to score a touchdown with the sermon." It was an excellent visual metaphor to help us frame our thinking about how worship was a narrative. Everything in worship was meant to "drive the ball down the field." This meant that the spoken word was connected to the music, the prayer, the scripture, tactile moments, graphics, and everything else we included in the experience. The sermon became the final chapter in a story that - after all of that buildup – people were eager to experience.

So how do you create a narrative? Here are four key questions to ask to help you design a more narrative worship experience:

1) WHAT IS YOUR DRIVING SCRIPTURE AND WHAT BIG IDEA DOES IT PRESENT?

What is the main idea for the scripture you are focused on? If you had to summarize it in a single phrase or sentence, what would it be? How can you then capture that idea in the music that you sing (regardless of style)? How can that scripture and its big idea be captured in the spoken word? What language can you bring to the prayer that ties back into the main idea? When crafting a children's sermon (if you do those), how can you create a distinct pathway into that big idea for children? When it comes to the adult sermon, how can you visit and revisit that biblical concept throughout? Finally, how can you tie your announcements into that big idea as well to create a more action-oriented experience?

When you consider how everything ties to the big narrative idea found in scripture, you'll create an experience that is cohesive and engaging. Worshipers both in the room and online will end the experience with more clarity. They're also much more likely to remember with greater detail what you talked about in that experience. When they think back on it, because they have a better memory of what you talked about, they're more likely to put it into practice. I'll add that the scripture should be the starting point, and it's why it's the first question to ask when creating a narrative experience. Don't start with the creative idea and find the scripture to match it. You run the risk of exegeting the scripture, and creating a memorable creative experience, in which the Gospel is lost in the creative gimmick.

2) WHAT IS THE FELT NEED THAT PEOPLE ARE WALKING IN OR TUNING IN WITH THAT RELATES TO THIS SCRIPTURE?

Worship planners have buzzed about "felt needs" based worship planning for decades. In my book, *Taking Flight with Creativity: Worship Design Teams That Work*, my co-author Len Wilson and I write about the importance of considering felt needs when designing worship in a collaborative process.[3]

The felt need approach encourages planners to take their best guess as to what participants may be feeling when confronting the driving scripture of the day. What does one feel as it relates to the biblical truth being presented? Without considering the felt needs that exist within participants on any given biblical topic, worship planners may inadvertently design an experience that flies right over the heads of worshipers. Or worship may just feel really out of touch. While not everyone shares the same felt need at the same time, determining what felt need a worship experience is speaking to gives focus to the planning. This clarity helps planners form narratives that are cohesive and compelling. For example, during a pandemic where many are out of work and struggling to make ends meet, a sermon series on stewardship is tricky. A non-felt need based approach would be to preach straight up principles on tithing.

Someone who has a job working as an entertainer, at a movie theater, or in a restaurant may not resonate with a sermon or worship experience that does not take into account the very real fears and challenges they're facing. A sermon that does not consider people in this situation might feel out of touch. That does not mean you shouldn't preach on tithing or stewardship. These are important biblical principles. Instead, when developing a sermon or service on this topic, after exegeting the scripture, wrestle with the felt need you're addressing, and how the two might come together. You will preach a different sermon and plan a different experience when you consider the felt needs of those you're trying to inspire into a life of stewardship.

3) WHAT IS YOUR "HOOK"? WHAT DOES THE BIG IDEA LOOK LIKE? WHAT IS THE STORY OR METAPHOR THAT YOU CAN HANG THIS TRUTH ON?

---

3. Len Wilson and Jason Moore, *Taking Flight with Creativity: Worship Design Teams That Work* (Nashville, TN: Abingdon Press, 2009.)

In television and movies, stories are often driven by what Alfred Hitchcock called a "MacGuffin." A MacGuffin is an object, device, or event that is necessary to the plot and the motivation of the characters, but insignificant, unimportant, or irrelevant in itself.[4] In other words, it's a metaphor, object, or story that propels the narrative forward. It makes the various characters, themes, and settings all work together. Think of the hook as a modern-day parable used to encapsulate your major biblical idea. It binds the various movements of worship together under one creative banner.

Referring to metaphor, marketing guru Seth Godin says, "The best way to learn a complex idea is to find it living inside something else you already understand." I like to think of this approach as creating "Modern Day Mustard Seed" moments. In the same way that Jesus picked up an ordinary object – insignificant, unimportant, and irrelevant in itself – and assigned new truth to it, we too can look for modern day equivalents to biblical themes. Jesus knew the people he was teaching would encounter the images he used again at a later time. He also knew that those images would bring those truths back, again and again. They would either create "ah-ha" moments or raise sacred questions that the listener (and viewer) would wrestle with long after the moment has passed.

Creative hooks are used all the time in visual storytelling. If you're a Marvel fan and you've watched WandaVision on Disney+, you will immediately recognize the hook it's hung on – the situation comedy. Each episode moves decade by decade through the various iterations of the sitcom. The story and characters are bound together by this hook. Or think back twenty years ago to Seinfeld, which made use of a hook in every episode of its "show about nothing." From the perilous "Soup Nazi," who required a certain restrictive method for ordering soup, to an entire episode where Jerry and his friends were waiting for a table at a Chinese restaurant, hooks brought everything together. Or maybe you were more of a Friends fan, and you remember the famous "PIVOT" episode where Chandler, Joey, and Ross tried to get a couch up the stairs to an apartment. Maybe that episode is a good metaphor for 2020/2021, where we all felt like we were uncomfortably pivoting with a heavy burden in an awkward space.

---

4. "MacGuffin," Wikipedia, accessed September 23, 2021, https://en.wikipedia.org/wiki/MacGuffin.

Establishing a creative hook can move you from disparate moments that feel like a variety show or pageant to a threaded narrative where all of the pieces fit together as one big story.

4) WHAT'S THE GOAL OF THIS EXPERIENCE?

Do you know what you'd like people to do as a result of the worship experience you're crafting? What's the action step you'd like them to take next when it's over? In advertising, that next step is often called the "call to action." The team I worked with at Ginghamsburg church called it "the desired outcome." We named it every time we planned worship. If you don't know the goal for your worship and what you hope people will take from it, there's a good chance that people who worship online and in-person will not know what to do with it.

Take the time to actually write it out, and make sure your team has consensus on each word you've written. A shared understanding of purpose is critical to creating worship that is cohesive. Is your goal a call to a specific mission project? Would you like them to get involved with a small group? Hope to help people heal? Want them to experience freedom in their finances? Answering this question in specific terms will help you create a better, more narrative experience that will be more likely to retain people until the end.

Now that we've explored both reimagining worship and reconceptualizing the experience of worship, in this next part of the book, we'll dig into three specific strategies for how to create Both/And hybrid worship. These will be achievable for churches of any size, worship style, comfort level with technology, and budget. They also work for churches that are rural, in the city, and everything in-between.

PART II
STRATEGIES FOR BOTH/AND WORSHIP

CHAPTER 3: PRE BOTH/AND WORSHIP

"How can I be in two places at once, unless I were a bird?"

-Boyle Roche

For those who were not streaming worship prior to the pandemic, being in two places at once was impossible. When Covid-19 prompted us to take the leap, everything changed. We didn't have to sprout wings and become a bird; we could be both online and in-person at the same time. Both/And worship in many ways evens the playing field for churches of all sizes, styles, and means. Even churches who do not have internet in their buildings can pull off the magic of being in two places at once by implementing one of three strategies. The first is what I call Pre Both/And worship.

WHAT IS PRE BOTH/AND WORSHIP?

Pre Both/And worship means worship is held as two completely separate experiences. The online experience is exclusively for those who are participating online, the in-person experience is for those in-person only, and never the twain shall meet. In this model, no streaming occurs. There is no need for cameras in the room. In other words, you are going to prerecord your worship for online and let that be the experience for the online congregation, and you're going to make the in-person experience more or less what it's always been in the past. The people in the room may never see a camera in the space, nor will they witness leaders trying to play to two audiences at once. This style of worship is Both/And, because you're serving each of your audiences (or congregations) in a way that gives them each your undivided attention. It can be – for many churches – the most intimate expression of worship because it allows the camera to get up close and personal.

Because you do not have to worry about blocking people in the room, the cameras can highlight fingers on keyboards and fretboards. The camera can be positioned directly in front of the leaders, and shots can be in motion without fear of distraction. Closer is always better for creating intimacy, and this model gives you lots of freedom to get as close as you want.

The church I attended as the pandemic began employed this approach. I am only an attendee of this church, not on staff. Because of my work on hybrid worship, the pastor at the time, lead pastor Jon Ferguson, would occasionally reach out to me for feedback or graciously listen to my critique as I had thoughts to share. The methodology that the team at Stillwater Church (near Dayton, Ohio) employed was shifted from a pre-pandemic livestreamed worship approach to a prerecorded/produced experience for online worship. Stillwater was streaming long before the pandemic began, but the leaders recognized that worship would need to be re-imagined to better serve folks not gathered in the building. Pastor Jon or associate pastor Jordan would come in on Saturday afternoon to record their sermons. Online pastor Andy Hill would record the message, positioning the camera mere feet away from whichever pastor was preaching. He would later edit the recordings, adding graphics and lower thirds as needed.

Stillwater offers a Saturday evening service, so the band was already in the rhythm of rehearsing for it. This allowed Andy to capture the final rehearsal of each song to be included in the prerecorded worship service. He had the freedom to move the camera around, capture closeups, and do things he would not have been able to do easily if there had been a room full of onlookers. Andy served not only as the camera operator and editor, but he was also the online worship host. This had him recording short segments to introduce the sermon series, encourage people to chat, give offering instructions, and generally begin and end each service. All of this happened through the week, and then on Saturday after recording the sermon and music, Andy would edit everything together and upload it to their preferred platform.

When it became safe to do so again, the church would meet in-person at 9:30 AM and 11:00 AM, and the online prerecorded service would air at those exact same times. You could either attend in-person at 9:30 AM or 11:00 AM, or you could worship online at these times. There were no cameras present in the room during in-person worship. This gave those worshiping online a wonderful experience of worship where they were the sole focus. Those in the room felt the same thing, as the leaders were speaking directly to them. It served both segments of the congregation in a way where neither felt like an afterthought.

With every form of Both/And worship, there are upsides and downsides that factor into which form is best for any given church. Here are the two sides of the coin a church must think about when considering Pre Both/And worship.

Let's start with the upsides:

1) MORE CONTROL OVER BOTH EXPERIENCES

Put simply, it's easier to do one thing at a time. This model allows you to light the room differently for prerecorded video and for live in-person worship. You can position the camera in the best place for intimacy and add graphics and video in a somewhat easier fashion. While you'll ultimately be in two places at once (on video and in person), you can maximize the experience for each respective audience.

2) LESS COMPROMISE AND ADAPTATION IS REQUIRED

If you'd like worship to feel a lot like it did pre-pandemic without having to give any consideration to how people online are experiencing it, this is the one for you. You don't have to compromise camera angles and shots, nor do you have to worry about the length of the service and a few other things we'll cover coming up.

3) YOU ONLY HAVE TO PREACH TO ONE AUDIENCE AT A TIME

It takes real work to preach to people both online and in the room at the same time. With this model, you don't have to. You preach to the camera for the prerecorded service, and you do what you more or less have always done with the in-person crowd.

4) YOU GET A SECOND TAKE

Have you ever been preaching or speaking in worship and had something come out of your mouth all wrong? Ever wish you could have a do-over? Well, when you prerecord, you have an opportunity to try it again. Take twos are possible when you are in Pre Both/And worship mode. Sometimes I wonder if this is an upside or a downside though. I am a perfectionist, and I often find myself doing way too many takes. I was invited to speak at a conference where I had a 25-minute keynote address to share, and it took me 2 hours to record it. If I had been live in the room, I would just have delivered my material and not worried about any flubbed words, pauses, and so on.

5) YOU CAN KILL TWO BIRDS WITH ONE STONE

As mentioned earlier, it's very important that we properly prepare for worship. Rehearsal should be required for all the worship we offer, whether in- person or online. I'm going to assume you'll take that to heart, and when you do, you can just record the last run through of the music piece, sermon, children's moment, or whatever aspect of worship you're prepping for your in-person gathering. Now you're ready for the live in-person experience, and you have what you need for the online experience.

6) TECHNOLOGY IS SIMPLER

When you're prerecording, you can have your camera directly in front of you without fear of blocking anyone. While I highly recommend using a wired mic, Bluetooth mic, or a direct feed from your soundboard, moving the camera closer (if you're using the onboard mic) does improve audio quality significantly. When the camera is closer, you can also hide lights just behind the view of the camera. Those can be pro lights with the ability to be dimmed or diffused, or they can even be lamps from your office or home. Either option will improve your shots dramatically.

When it comes to streaming live, there are three factors you have limited control over: the upstream, the platform, and the downstream. When it comes to prerecording, you get to eliminate two of them.

First is the upstream. This is the connection at your house, church, or wherever you're broadcasting from. If this stream isn't fast, its signal experiences interference, or the bandwidth is overloaded because people in the building are on the network, things can stutter, lose sync, and fail completely. With Pre Both/And worship, you don't have to worry about that. When you prerecord, it doesn't matter how long it takes to upload, so long as it's online before you want to premiere it.

The second factor is the platform. There are several popular platforms for streaming worship online. Among the most popular are Facebook, YouTube, Vimeo, Zoom, and LifeChurch.tv's "Church Online Platform." I know a few pastors streaming on Twitch as well. The ability to stream on each of these platforms is great, especially given that they're all free to use.

The downside is that sometimes they get overwhelmed by too much traffic, and they can slow down. This was especially true during the first couple of weeks of the pandemic. Reports came in all over the nation from pastors who lost a stream in the middle of the service, lost their audio, had glitchy playback, or had long lags. None of these platforms were ready for the bandwidth onslaught caused by so many churches jumping online at once.

With Pre Both/And worship, you have a much lower risk of having the platform choke on you during your stream. It's not impossible, but it's less likely. When you upload a video for premiere, the platform has time to chew on that data and compress it for better playback, resulting in a more stable stream. When you're streaming in real time, the platform is doing all of the work on the fly to receive, convert, and then downstream that data.

The final factor is the downstream. When someone is streaming your worship from their device, be it a smart TV, tablet, or cell phone, they're on the downstream side of this three-part equation. Unfortunately, there's not a lot you can do about how fast their connection is. The other two factors are largely eliminated with Pre Both/And, but this one is what it is.

There are also some downsides to Pre Both/And worship, as there are with every form of hybrid experiences. You can weigh these against the other two forms and see which is the best option for your specific context. Here are some of the drawbacks:

1) MORE PEOPLE MAY NEED TO BE INVOLVED

Creating a fully prerecorded and edited worship experience is a big task with multiple steps involved. Teams must plan, rehearse, film, edit, add additional media (lyrics, graphics and video), and then upload it all to the platform. Shots often look better when they're composed by someone sitting on the other side of the camera. Lighting is hard to adjust when you can't see the frame, and monitoring audio is really hard to do alone. Not every church has a team, let alone a staff member to do all of this work. It is worth getting creative though to recruit others to help in these various tasks. If you have a college near you with a communications program, you might explore setting up an internship. Or nowadays there are a lot of high schools that have media arts programs running where students learn rudimentary editing, photo manipulation, and more. This was true for my son Ethan who, at the time of this writing, was entering his sophomore year of high school. Last year, his class tackled basic Photoshop editing, video editing, and even a little bit of html coding. Students like my son often have an aptitude for technical things. Consider that students (whether in high school or college) who are studying communications and media design often love to play with the tools. They want to try out their skills with a real audience. There's nothing better for an artist than seeing their work displayed on a screen with a room full of people, or in this case, an audience streaming online. Also, many students are broke and would very likely show up weekly to record and edit for a very small investment from your church. My son, who doesn't have a driver's license or a job yet, would see $25 to $50 a week as a goldmine. If you offered the equivalent of a decent meal out after church as a weekly stipend, you'd not only get his attention, but you might just help him find a calling that would last the rest of his life. Where might you recruit a young person to help ease your burden, but also empower them to lead?

One quick side note for pastors: I just want to acknowledge all of the extra work you've been doing since Covid-19 shut the world down. You didn't go to seminary to learn to exegete scripture in order to write sermons that you then had to learn and internalize, only to have to film, then edit, and upload online. I've heard more than one pastor say that he didn't go to seminary to become a video producer, and I completely feel for anyone who feels overwhelmed by all of this. If you're still struggling, start building a volunteer team, even if you have to pay them a little. Your church needs you! Burnout is real, and pastors who are doing it all are experiencing burnout right now on a daily basis.

2) FURTHER PLANNING IS REQUIRED

This one is a downside for some, and not even a consideration for others. In my twenty plus years in ministry, I've worked with pastors who both plan a year out at a time, and others who sweat their way through regularly occurring "Saturday night specials." If you're one of those "the-Holy-Spirit-always-gives-me-my-sermon-on-Saturday-night" preachers, Pre Both/And is going to require you to negotiate with the Spirit for a little more advanced notice. You can't really write a sermon at the last minute and then film, edit, and upload without losing a lot of impact in the process. If you're working with others to achieve Pre Both/And worship, the last minute stuff can tax your team and create resentments that can tear good volunteers apart. Honor your team and your congregation by giving yourself enough time to write, learn, shoot, edit, and upload worship that doesn't feel thrown together. The Spirit can and does show up before Saturday night, I promise.

3) EQUIPMENT AND SOFTWARE HAS A LEARNING CURVE

Remember in *The Matrix*, when Neo learned Kung-Fu three seconds after it was uploaded to his brain? Unfortunately, software and hardware don't come that easily. Even with a plethora of free tutorials on YouTube, it takes time to learn how to shoot, light, and mic good video. Editing can move from being utilitarian in its approach to highly artistic, but it takes time to get there. This is where having a team alleviates some of the stress solo producers feel when going it alone. By now, if you've been at this since 2020, you've probably got a decent handle on it, but there's always more to learn.

KEY CONSIDERATIONS FOR PRE BOTH/AND WORSHIP

Creating a transcendent experience of worship that is prerecorded requires some rethinking of what worship looks like. Here are a few considerations to think about with this particular strategy.

Service Length

As I stated earlier, when it comes to lone worship, shorter is better. I believe that Nona's recommendations are accurate when she tells us 25-40 minutes is the sweet spot for online worship. Since this strategy has you offering two distinct experiences, (a prerecorded online and a live in-person) you really can create a Both/And win.

With this model, you don't have to compromise the length of your in-person experience at all. Do what you've always done. If it was an hour before, it can be an hour again. Be mindful though that, if you shortened in-person at all during the pandemic, going back may be a challenge. You've altered expectations, so be strategic about the shift back.

For online prerecorded worship, you may need to make some tough choices on what to include and exclude, but when you hit that 25-40 minute mark, you're golden.

Singing

We've already established that singing doesn't really work as well online as it does in-person. This is one area where less is more, and if you're trying to cut your length, music is one of the ways to lessen the total. If you do traditional music, you might reduce the number of verses you do in each hymn. If you're doing non-traditional music, you may reduce the number of songs you offer during this time.

At the church I was attending during the pandemic, Andy Hill would record all of the songs the team would be doing in the live services the following day. He'd then include just one or two of those in the prerecorded version that was streamed online. I know that this is a hard one for some to swallow - especially musicians – but there is a win-win opportunity you might also consider when it comes to how to present the music online. You might also record the entire song set you're offering in the room (either as a rehearsal or during the live worship) and then post it to the platforms you stream on as a separate video file. The whole song set from the in-person worship can go on Facebook and YouTube with relatively no effort.

You might say in your prerecorded service, "Today we've included some of the music we're singing in our in-person service, and if you love to worship in song, you can check out the entire set that has been posted to our Facebook (and/or YouTube) page." You can also make the invitation to the online community to come to in-person worship to experience the entire set live as it's happening. What you're essentially doing when you only include some of the music in your prerecorded worship, while then posting the whole set separately, is allowing people to opt into the music. Rather than taking the risk of losing them by doing a long set up front where they may disconnect, you give them the option to participate on their own accord.

Now, I recognize that every church's context is different. If you find that music transcends the technology at your church, you may choose to continue the entire thing, but take the time to ask around and see what you can learn about participation from home. It's a hard reality to face, but you may find that people aren't really singing all that much.

Sermon

If we're following Nona Jones' recommendations of 25-35 minutes with a maximum of 40 minutes, you have to cut in multiple places. The sermon is one of them.

As stated, when it comes to online worship, our attention spans are shorter. This is partly because the opportunity for distraction is higher in an environment where we have no control. It's hard to stay focused sitting in a living room as opposed to sitting in a sanctuary or auditorium. How long is your typical sermon? Twenty-five minutes? Forty-five? An hour? Simply put, you can't do a thirty-five-minute sermon and a forty-minute service. That's called a sermon. You can't do a twenty-five-minute sermon and a thirty-minute service. That's also called a sermon. Whatever length you're used to doing in-person in the pre-pandemic era, there's a pretty good bet it should be reduced for online. But by how much? Consider the TED talk model.

If you've never heard of TED talks, today is the day to take your first steps into a larger world! TED stands for Technology, Entertainment, and Design. TED talks create buzz. They're punchy and inspiring. They don't waste words. Many go viral. The maximum length of a TED talk is 18 minutes. It doesn't matter if you're a largely unknown entity or whether you're Bill Gates, everyone gets a maximum of 18 minutes. Many TED talks are shorter. But why? TED curator Chris Anderson explained the organization's thinking this way:

> It [18 minutes] is long enough to be serious and short enough to hold people's attention. It turns out that this length also works incredibly well online. It's the length of a coffee break. So, you watch a great talk, and forward the link to two or three people. It can go viral, very easily. The 18-minute length also works much like the way Twitter forces people to be disciplined in what they write. By forcing speakers who are used to going on for 45 minutes to bring it down to 18, you get them to really think about what they want to say. What is the key point they want to communicate? It has a clarifying effect. It brings discipline.[1]

---

1. Carmine Gallo, "The Science Behind TED's 18-Minute Rule", Linkedin, published March 13, 2014, https://www.linkedin.com/pulse/20140313205730-5711504-the-science-behind-ted-s-18-minute-rule.

What makes TED talks so effective? Forbes author Carmine Gallo analyzed over 500 talks and found three key factors:

> ***1) Emotion: Ideas that spread touch our hearts***
>
> In order for persuasion to occur, you must touch a person's heart before reaching their head. The most popular TED speakers connect with audiences on a deeply emotional level primarily because they're storytellers...
>
> The best storytellers also use humor, exude commanding body language, and incorporate animated verbal delivery. Above all, they are passionate about their topic; passionate to the point of obsession.
>
> ***2) Novelty: Ideas that spread teach us something new***
>
> ...According to Dr. A. K. Pradeep, "Our brains are trained to look for something brilliant and new, something that stands out, something that looks delicious."
>
> Ideas stick when they are packaged as new, surprising, and unexpected—something 'delicious'...
>
> When the brain detects something unexpected or surprising, it immediately says, "Oh, here's something new. I'd better pay attention."
>
> The chemical dopamine is released which acts as your brain's natural "save button." Dopamine is so important to retention and learning that when it's present, we tend to remember an experience or a message. When it's absent, nothing seems to stick.
>
> Novelty is the single most effective way to capture a person's attention.
>
> ***3) Memorable: Ideas that spread are easy to recall***
>
> Lackluster content will leave your audience bored, but a memorable presentation is one your audience is much more likely to share long after your presentation is over.
>
> The best TED speakers make their presentations memorable by doing the following:
>
> -Use pictures instead of text on their slides whenever possible (picture superiority).

-Rely on the rule of three to deliver their content (three stories, three parts, etc.)[2]

-Focus on one key theme, the "one thing" they want the audience to know…

I'm encouraging every pastor to consider creating a TED talk-style sermon for their Pre Both/And worship. How can you follow the best practices above when writing your 18-minutes-or-less sermon? If this makes you nervous, remember with Pre Both/And worship, you can still do your full-length sermon in person. For the online audience, shorten it up, and make it punchy and poignant.

Here's another idea to consider; in addition to posting your condensed sermon with your 40-minutes-or-less worship service to Facebook or YouTube, post the sermon as a separate video as well. This makes it easily sharable by your people. It's much harder for those inspired by your sermon to share it on their timelines when it's encapsulated within a 40-minute service. Enthusiastic parishioners who want to share your brilliant sermon would have to say something like, "My pastor had a great sermon today, check it out. You'll find the sermon 15 minutes into this video. It goes until about 35 minutes in. Don't miss it!" That's way too cumbersome, and very few people are going to watch if they have to dig around to find it. Instead, if they can just post the sermon all by itself – in the same way a TED talk can be shared - then who knows? I'd love to believe our sermons could go viral.

Call to Action

Lastly, we might also consider what the "call to action" is for those tuning into both our prerecorded and in-person gatherings of worship. "Call to action" is a popular buzz phrase used in business to identify what entrepreneurs hope a customer will do after encountering a website, commercial, or advertisement. What do you want people to do as a result of the worship you're crafting? If we don't give people something to do or a way to engage in our Both/And expressions of worship, we miss a huge opportunity.

2. Carmine Gallo, "TED Talks Are Wildly Addictive for Three Powerful Scientific Reasons," *Forbes*, February 25, 2014, https://www.forbes.com/sites/carminegallo/2014/02/25/ted-talks-are-wildly-addictive-for-three-powerful-scientific-reasons/?sh=37d770546b6a.

This is why I'm so passionate about moving from announcements to action steps. When crafted to be an extension of the sermon, that information becomes a valuable next step for participants.

We must think about what active participation looks like in this new era of hybrid ministry. People should feel like they're a part of it, even when it's prerecorded. That only happens when we are intentional about crafting moments of participation, using specific language, and making extensive use of chat and other two-way forms of communication like texts and Zoom.

In my Both/And webinar, I show a short excerpt from a traditional worship experience featuring my friend Rev. Ben Gosden on a week they prerecorded worship. In the clip, Ben starts off by telling his congregation that they have prerecorded that day's service. He starts by saying, "Friends, this week we have prerecorded worship service, which means through the magic of the internet, I am in two places at once. I'm here before you now, but I'm also with you in the chat on Facebook. This morning as I'm praying, I want to invite you to share your prayer concerns live in the chat. You can list the things you're grateful for, but also share the things that you might want us to pray for too. Today I will be live commenting right along with you as you participate in the chat. Think of typing your concerns in as praying along with us. Let us go to the Lord now in prayer." He then begins praying, leaving space for people to enter their concerns digitally.

In these moments, Ben is calling his people to action. Even though it's recorded, the interaction is live, creating an experience that transcends the technology and even the fact that it's recorded.

A pastor I began coaching in 2021, Rev. Karen Gygax Rodriguez (The Federated Church of Green Lake), includes questions in her prerecorded worship that she actively responds to in real time via chat. On the Sunday I was in-person to visit her church for a consultation, in their prerecorded worship (one of three worship forms they offer – two live, one prerecorded), Karen asked what people were thankful for. One person immediately typed in "fresh strawberries". Karen responded by saying, "I love strawberries." Another participant piped in saying, "I have a wonderful strawberry pie recipe." Yet another said, "Oh I want that recipe." The conversation continued from there.

Karen had thoughtfully and artfully left space in the prerecording to let the conversation happen within the chat. It was a wonderful thing to experience as I was participating in the prerecorded online worship as it was premiering.

When people are engaging and interacting in chat, they are active participants, not passive watchers of worship. They are not spectators or observers, but active members of the congregation.

ENCOURAGE PARTICIPATION

So how do we get people to participate both in person and online? It's a question I often get from group cohort sessions I lead. It's tricky at first. In in-person worship, depending on your faith tradition, you may be encouraged to shout out a joy or concern in real time. You may also be invited to "pass the peace" or greet a neighbor. In some traditions, there is an anticipated "call and response" aspect to the worship experience. Participation in these churches is the name of the game. In other churches, some may be reticent to talk out loud. They may not lean in to participation.

Getting people to participate can be challenging in both in-person and online worship, but participation via chat can also open up new possibilities for dynamic interactions in both in-person and online worship. For some of us it's a brand new way of thinking. The technology that allows us to participate in the online experience when we're not in the building can also be a vehicle for connection to those outside the sanctuary and others who may be worshiping away from us online. Chat is an excellent way to connect.

Consider however that people have always been discouraged from talking in church, so in some ways we've discouraged participation. Turning on a phone in worship has always been frowned upon. This may have shifted slightly in the last few years as more and more people read scripture off a Bible app, but there are still seasoned (or salty may be a better word) congregants who scowl at those with phones out in church. Our phones are a portal to the experience, and a wonderful way to connect. It's time we begin to reframe our thinking around them and lean into what that they can do for interaction and community building, but we're going to have to teach our congregants how.

Here are three things we can do to encourage online chat participation in worship and at home.

1) GIVE THEM PERMISSION

To create a culture of participation, you must go out of your way to give permission. Normalize it. Refer to it often. Will some people play Candy Crush? Yes. But before that they may have doodled on an offering envelope or counted ceiling tiles. People who are distracted have had options long before we had smartphones.

2) TEACH THEM HOW

Since this is new territory for many, a good tutorial goes a long way in encouraging participation. Tell them how to navigate to chat and open it if they haven't already. Use a QR code in print on screen for easy access. Teach them how to send hearts and likes in the moment.

3) PRIME THE PUMP

When it comes to interactivity, nobody wants to go first. I've led dozens of Zoom meetings as a follow up to my Both/And webinars. I start with two questions: 1) What is something you've tried since the training a month ago and did it work or not? and 2) What is something you're excited about in ministry that didn't exist prior to the pandemic?

The first 15 seconds is always awkward. Nobody wants to talk. I've had 65 people in a Zoom room, and there's not a raised hand anywhere to be found – and these are pastors! They love to talk. When I say, "This session is all about you talking, not me," someone usually hits the raise hand button and then shares the answer to one of the two questions I posed. Once someone breaks the ice, it's not long before the second and third persons are ready to jump in. From there a queue line starts forming. After that it's hard to end on time. This same thing can happen in our online chat. You ask a question, and no one answers. It's easy to give up quickly thinking, "My people just don't participate." Maybe it's just that no one wants to go first.

Years ago, I was speaking at an event with Dr. Leonard Sweet. I got to know Len back in the 1990s, and we formed a lasting friendship. On several occasions I've had the opportunity to both speak alongside him, but also "video veejay" for him. Basically, I have been allowed to visually illustrate what he's talking about in real time on the screens behind him as he's teaching. This could be pulling up images from Google on the fly, creating some original graphics ahead of time, or using something he provided to me beforehand. One such example of this is a video titled: "First Follower: Leadership Lessons from Dancing Guy."

You can find the video here:
https://youtu.be/fW8amMCVAJQ

In the three-minute clip, a shirtless man dances wildly in the middle of a crowd. From the looks of it, no one is really paying much attention to him. This guy has the guts to look silly in a crowd and do his own thing. Twenty seconds in, another young man – this one with a shirt – joins into this wacky dance. The leader acknowledges him, and the solo dance becomes a duet. They continue to dance inviting others in, and eventually a second follower turns the duet into a trio. The three of them dance together swinging their arms around, jumping up and down, and rolling on the ground – they're having a great time. A few moments pass, and two more dancers enter the scene, and seconds later three more join in. Momentum builds as the dance party expands exponentially. As the narrator Derek Sivers says, "As more people jump in, it's no longer risky. If they were on the fence before, there's no reason to not jump in now. They won't stand out, they won't be ridiculed and they'll be part of the in-crowd if they hurry." The next moments see almost the entire crowd join the dance. They run from their seated positions to jump in as quickly as possible. Now there's pressure to join the crowd, because the tables have turned and to not dance means you're in the minority.[3]

What we can learn from this video is that it's hard to go first, easier to go second, and progressively easier to join the crowd. If we foster a culture of interactivity, people will strongly desire to be a part of it. I'd encourage you to have some "plants" ready to prime the pump. If you're going to ask a reflection question, recruit a few people to think on it throughout the week and ask them to commit to sharing their reflection in the chat when you go live. In time, you will find that people are drawn to interactivity and will see it as an essential part of the experience.

ONLINE WORSHIP CAN BE EVERGREEN WORSHIP

One of the greatest aspects of worship going online because of the pandemic is that worship now has a life that has the potential to live well

3. Derek Sivers, "First Follower: Leadership Lessons from Dancing Guy," YouTube, February 11, 2010, https://www.youtube.com/watch?v=fW8amMCVAJQ.

beyond the moment. It's incredible now to think about how prior to the pandemic, so much energy and effort was put into an experience that lasted for an hour (more or less, depending on context), and when it was over, it was over. The only people who benefitted from it were the people that showed up that day.

Now worship can live on, long into the future.

People who participate in worship weeks, months, and years later can have a transformational experience if we craft online worship in such a way that gives some attention to language and how things work or don't work beyond the moment we're living in when we offer it.

Failure to bring evergreen language to prerecorded (and even real- time worship) embeds within the experience a shelf life that will create disconnects to online viewers. Evergreen language is important in both Pre Both/And worship, and Real Time Both/And worship, and many of these lessons apply to both forms. Here we'll focus primarily on Pre Both/And.

Intentional Language

Language matters, and our language for in-person worship will sound very different than it does with the prerecroded worship. With this model, your language in the room (because you are not streaming) can look the way it always has. You don't have to think about the online language at all in the in-person worship.

When we build action and participation into the prerecorded experience of worship, we must be mindful of the language we're using both in that experience of worship and behind the scenes when we're planning it too. Language can both reflect and shape our ideology about worship.

Because online worship happens on screens, it's easy for us to fall into language often associated with screens. The words "watching" and "viewing" are often used in relation to digital forms of worship. We need better/more accurate language when describing the worship that we're offering for an online audience. We should eliminate "watching" and "viewing" from our vocabulary. Instead, consider adopting "worshiping" and "participating" as we describe what is happening in online worship. Now, that assumes that you're creating actual space for people to really interact and participate. When we engage people with interactivity, they go from passive watchers to active worshipers – from viewers to participants.

Delayed Viewing

In my consultation work and through my seminars, I've been hearing many churches say that their live worship numbers have dropped, but on delay or on demand worship numbers have risen. The way we consume content in the world outside of church has changed dramatically even in the last half decade. The rise of Netflix, Amazon Prime Video, Disney+, Apple TV, and other streaming options has turned us into a "watch-it-when-we-wanna" society.

In an article on *The Wrap*, dated February 17, 2021, it was announced that three of "the big four" major television networks were "swearing off Nielsen's Live + Same Day TV ratings." CBS, whose viewers skew oldest, is the one holdout clinging to the old system. The Nielsen ratings have been the measure of success for tv shows since the 1950s. In a stunning announcement, Stuart Levine, VP of Editorial and Media Relations, Entertainment Networks, NBCUniversal Television and Streaming, wrote,

> Dear TV Writers:
>
> We wanted to alert you that this week will mark the end of the fast affiliate ratings email you receive in the morning.
>
> We didn't come to this decision lightly, but believe it's important to accurately reflect how the television business is changing and, specifically, how these early ratings numbers are no longer representative of the performance of a particular show or series.
>
> Long gone are the days when a vast majority of viewers watched their favorite shows in the exact timeslot in which they were scheduled. And as a business, we are much more focused on how audiences are watching our shows rather than when audiences are watching our shows, which could be different depending on the genre and demographics of any given series. [4]

Our viewing habits have changed with television, and now even with movies that are being released the same day in theaters and online. What implications does this shift have on worship? How can we measure success

4. Tony Maglio, "NBC Joins Fox and ABC in Ditching Nielsen's Live + Same Day TV Ratings: CBS Is the Last One Standing," *The Wrap*, February 17, 2021, https://www.thewrap.com/nbc-tv-ratings-live-same-day-stop-abc-fox/.

when it's not just about "butts in seats"? New metrics need to be developed. Maybe professions of faith, baptisms, giving, discipleship participation, and mission are all better measurables anyway, but I'll leave that to the bean counters.

While there were many early adopters who were online before Covid-19, the dramatic uptick caused by the pandemic means that people can engage in new ways with our worship. Worship "on-demand" is here to stay. It's an incredible shift. And by the way – I've been hearing about churches who are claiming they have "binge watchers" who now worship at multiple recorded services in a row. What a great time it is to be the church!

Worship used to happen at a certain time and a certain place. We had all the control on those two factors. The pandemic took them away from us, and now people can "consume" worship in an entirely different way than before. They can choose when, where, and how much they watch. They can do it from their living room on any day they want, at any time they want, and they can skip past the parts they don't really like. This is why creating a powerful narrative is so important. Disparate pieces are much easier to skip past.

Because people are worshiping on delay, there are minor moments of disconnect that can arise if we're not careful about our temporal language. For instance, saying "Good morning, we hope you're having a great Sunday," creates a minor disconnect for someone watching on a Wednesday afternoon during their lunch break. Instead, we might say, "Welcome to worship, we hope you're having a great day." A small language tweak can have a real impact. Even if it's largely subliminal.

It is important that we begin giving what I call an "evergreen content pass" to the worship we create. As you are planning, ask if there's anything you're saying in the moment that is not going to make sense if it comes up in a YouTube search in six months.

Temporal Language

Temporal language can kill the feeling of connection someone might have when watching on delay. Sometimes there's a sort of shorthand that is used for the in-person crowd that may not make sense later when watching on delay. For example, you might say something like, "Friends, as we move through the day tomorrow, we must remember what an important day it is. Reflect on all that people went through and the struggles they faced. Be mindful all throughout this day of remembrance." You might be thinking, what day are you talking about? Well, if you don't capture what's happening in that moment for posterity's sake, the people who are watching on delay will be wondering that, too. These might be the kinds of words you'd offer on the Sunday preceding Martin Luther King Jr. observance day. Without giving words to that specific event, your on-delay crowd could be completely lost. Capture what is happening in the moment. Give record to it. Be careful of using shorthand language that favors the real-time room.

Temporal language can pull people who watch on delay out of the moment. Instead of saying, "Good morning, welcome to worship. I hope you're having a great Sunday," say, "Welcome to worship, I hope you're having a great day." Someone who may be watching your worship during their lunch break on Monday afternoon will experience less disconnect when avoiding the temporal language.

Posterity

In February of 2021, I offered my Both/And webinar to the Central Texas Conference of The United Methodist Church. I shared this idea of "evergreen content" with the group on that day. During my 30-day follow-up, one church admitted to me that they didn't really get it or the importance of evergreen content, that is, until they went back to review their worship a couple of weeks later.

The day I offered the training, there was a freak ice storm that hit Texas hard. While ice storms are not unheard of in Texas, this was an unusual winter blast that brought down ice and snow, making roads treacherous to travel on and freezing just about everything one could imagine. During this particular week, the aforementioned church told me, their pipes froze and burst, causing flooding throughout the building. That Sunday morning, caution signs, "slippery when wet" warnings, and fans working overtime to dry out carpets, were positioned throughout the building. The people who attended in-person walked past those devices and signs to enter the worship space. Online, people who were watching in real time from the local community had witnessed that same weather system. They had been dealing with it too.

Throughout worship, leaders casually referenced the flood, the fans, and all of the things working to rectify this unfortunate reality. Upon the review of their worship, they realized that they never really explained what had happened that weekend. The offhand comments about the flood that frequently were brought up never mentioned the incident that brought about the frozen pipes and the flood that followed. An on-delay watcher tuning in months later might think the sermon is about Noah with all this talk about the flood. You don't have to tell the people in the room about the flood; they know. The people on delay need you to walk them through it in order to capture the moment for posterity, so they understand the reference.

A simple spoken moment up front could make all the difference. You might say, "Friends, it's been a challenging week here at our church. We had unusual weather hit us hard and we've had frigid temps, freezing rain, and snow. Our pipes burst, so here in the building we're dealing with the aftermath of a flood."

This kind of intro allows you to include the on-delay watchers and gives them the necessary info to make sense of whatever shorthand you'd use following it.

Re-cap Language

Another consideration for evergreen content that those who preach in a series must think about is recap language. You can't count on the fact that your online people watched last week or the weeks prior. If you are building on content from week to week, you have to walk people to where you've been to catch them up to where you're going. Use the "previously on" model you see on most TV programs. At the start of nearly every television program you hear "previously on" spoken, followed by a swiftly edited clip of moments from earlier in the season that catch you up to what's about to happen.

What you don't want a first-time guest to experience is you saying, "You all remember when I talked about my vacation last week and what went down there? It's kinda like that." If they weren't there or haven't watched that week's video, they have no clue what you're referring to. If it's their first time, they're not likely to go digging through your other videos to figure out when last week was.

Naming Your Stream

Last, when it comes to the evergreen nature of worship that is archived, naming it properly is of utmost importance. I've seen way too many churches name their online service "Month, day, year, Name of church." In other words, "January 10, 2022, Acme Church Worship." Naming your service by the date instantly gives it a shelf life that doesn't last as long. It feels old the very next week. Also, no one is searching the date and the name of your church except for maybe your people. Instead, as my friend Pastor Chris Winterman says, "Create a clickbait title to draw them in." What felt need are you trying to hit? Start there. A title like "Finding Your Faith in a Season of Fear" is going to be way more clickable than the date and the name of your church. Even better is, "I'm Scared, Does God Even Care?" Give them a reason to click.

Building Meaningful Relationships

I believe the key to sustainability for both the in-person and online forms of Both/And worship is relationship building. Although it's much easier to build relationships in our physical spaces than it is online, it is completely possible and necessary to do so online too.

One of the best ways for us to build relationships through online worship is to have a dedicated worship host. A worship host can be clergy or laity. He or she becomes like an ambassador to the online community, welcoming them in, making them feel comfortable, setting expectations, and making sure all the pieces come together. These folks talk directly to people worshiping online and make them feel included. Having a worship host present in a chat should be a non-negotiable. I recommend them being on camera as well, but let's focus first on what they bring to chat.

Worship Hosts and Greeters as Chat Hosts

If you're not already doing so, think of chat as a virtual welcome center (or what some call a narthex). It's a place to greet people by name, answer questions they might have, encourage participation, and is an opportunity to reinforce everything taking place in worship. This can be staffed by volunteers from home or in person. You can also pull from your existing hospitality team. Ask your greeters to greet in the chat instead of at the door. Here are some ways to use the chat:

OFFER WELCOME:

Use the chat to greet each person by name. As they come in, say hello. Tell them it's good to see them. Do what you'd do if you were a greeter at the door.

TAKE QUESTIONS:

Remember that with online worship, you have a lot of new eyes and ears on your worship. There may be things we do that outsiders do not know how to do or may not understand the meaning of. Ask if they have questions, and maybe even be proactive in giving short explanations of things that might feel like a "secret handshake" to outsiders.

One church I worked with would post one or two sentence descriptions of some of the movements of worship and would define words like "sacrament," "eucharist," and even "connect card." Don't assume people know the drill.

REINFORCE EVERYTHING:

The chat is a great backup for the sermon and other aspects of worship. I've been encouraging churches since almost the beginning of the pandemic to prepare a document ahead of time that you can copy and paste right into the chat.

If your pastor is a "3 point preacher," post each point as he or she offers them verbally. Post the scripture references too. If there are quotes used from authors or leaders, or even great quotes from the pastor that happen in the sermon, put them in the chat.

There's a balance to find here. Too much may be distracting, but in the same way, churches with screens use them to reinforce the sermon and other pieces in the room. We can reinforce those things in the chat as well.

POST LINKS:

Ultimately when it comes to worship, we want people to act. We want them to get involved in that Bible study, go on that mission trip, give to the offering, and so on. Make it as easy as possible by posting links in the chat as they're mentioned.

These can go in that same document you prepare ahead of time for the sermon material. The moment something is mentioned in an announcement, during offering, or in the sermon, post the link so that participants can act right away.

FOSTER REFLECTION:

Interactivity is one of the best things of all about Both/And worship. We can now have a sense of what people are thinking and feeling throughout the experience. We can also challenge people to chew on things in the moment that may bring about a more meaningful experience for them and others who may be observing their reflections.

As part of your planning for each week of worship, consider writing a reflection question to be included in the chat at the beginning of the experience. In Pre Both/And worship, you'll be limited to seeing and responding to those questions in chat, because the sermon has already been recorded, but in Real Time Both/And worship, you can save room in the sermon to mention some of them during the livestream.

Either way, this kind of interactivity keeps people not worshiping in the building feeling like they're part of the worship experience. There's nothing like seeing your comment responded to by the pastor and other leaders to make a worshiper feel valued and included.

INVITE FOLLOW-UP:

If we're not intentional about relationship building, our online experiences of worship will become a revolving door where people will come in and leave without us ever knowing. We can use the chat to send them to an online form to register their attendance (what many call a connect card). We can also use services like "Text in Church," which allows participants to text in "Imhere" or "new" to start an automated process of follow-up.

You can get a free 60-day trial of their pro membership here:

http://bit.ly/TextInChurchFreeOffer.

And if you offer a first-time visitor/guest gift in the building, offer that to onliners too. Tell them they can come by the church to pick it up or offer to put one in the mail. Or even better yet, create a digital first-time visitor/guest gift like a Red Box code, Starbucks gift code, or some other gift equivalent to what you would have given them if they'd come in-person.

A robust chat experience is a catalyst to creating real and lasting relationships with worshipers not physically present. If you haven't already built a team for this purpose, today's the day to start. Think of this as similar to building a team of greeters and ushers, only now the hospitality is being extended digitally.

Let's shift to what an on-camera host brings to the experience. This is a huge asset in the effort to build meaningful relationships.

On-Camera Hosts

When the pandemic began, the church I was attending at the time went "all in" on the worship host concept. By June they had hired a part-time online worship host named Andy Hill. Prior to that, the church's part-time social media/children's ministry assistant had done her best with a busy schedule. Later the already taxed for time lead pastor Jon Ferguson and associate pastor Jordan Wilson were doing the editing for the online service each week. Andy's presence, both on-camera and off, brought about a wonderful new dynamic to the worship experience that was palpable for the home audience right from the beginning. He made you feel like you were a part of it, even when worshiping from home.

In my webinar, I share a clip from a typical Pre Both/And experience at the church where Andy served. He starts off with a verbal self-introduction as a lower third graphic appears on screen. His name and title are on it. After welcoming the online congregation to the worship experience, he recaps the current series they're in. He then prefaces the message that pastor Jon will offer in a few moments. From there, Andy invites those in the chat to welcome one another and fill out the online connect card so that the church can stay in touch. He then invites people to give to the offering in one of three ways (mail, church app, or website). From there, Andy sets up a pre-produced video to celebrate veterans on this Veterans Day weekend.

I love sharing this clip for multiple reasons. It demonstrates the ROI I mentioned earlier, it shows the importance of teaching people how to give, encourages participation and connection in the chat, and it sets the tone for the rest of the service. Best of all, it's not super fancy. Andy records these hosting pieces on a smartphone with a ring light from a room in his home. He's not even mic'd up. It may not be the highest end production, but it's very effective. As stated, authenticity is more important than being slick.

What makes for a good online/on-camera worship host? Here's a checklist to consider:

ARTICULATE:

The person who is representing your church online has a big responsibility. He or she is ushering people into an encounter with the living God. If your host can't find words or stumbles a lot when speaking, he or she may not be the best selection for this role. This person should be able to wield words with ease and skill.

COMFORTABLE ON CAMERA:

A person can be extremely articulate and completely uncomfortable on camera. This may lead to freezing up, making it hard to get through a take. That little red tally light can mess with one's head. As a video producer, I've seen it happen numerous times over the years, often with very articulate people. When selecting a worship host be sure they feel comfortable on camera.

UNDERSTAND TECHNOLOGY:

While a worship host does not have to be a techno wiz, he or she does need to have some degree of technical know-how. Is the camera pointed in the right direction? Is the shot in focus? Is the lighting okay? Is the mic plugged in? If you have a team, your on-camera host may not have to be as concerned with these questions, but many churches have just one person doing it all.

IN THE KNOW:

The worship host needs to be included in and made aware of the plan for the entire experience. They are the glue that makes everything hang together. Your host's verbal transitions from one element of worship to another are critical in creating a cohesive experience. Pastors, worship leaders, children's ministers, and other leaders should communicate with the worship host about the things they're offering so that transitions can be made smoothly. In a Pre Both/And model, the hosting segments can be scripted and recorded with the other pieces in mind. In Real Time Both/And services, there may be more ad-libbing and improvisation happening live and in the moment. Knowing what's happening throughout is critical for those moments where the host must vamp.

AVAILABLE AND WILLING TO CONNECT WITH WORSHIPERS:

An online worship host is not just an on-camera personality. The host is like the "worship pastor" for the online congregation. The time on-camera is a great first step to relationship building, but what happens in the chat and through text, Zoom, and other means is where the real work is done.

When prerecording, chat is the only way to interact in real time. Worship hosts might consider following the chat recommendations made earlier. They should be active throughout the experience, getting to know worshipers through interactivity.

Over time, the online congregation will come to know the worship host as their pastor, even if they're a layperson. There is a high level of comfort found in that familiar face, presentation style, and voice each week.

The role of worship host can be filled by more than one person. The downside of it being just one person is that they may eventually get burnt out. It's also potentially jarring for the online audience if, for a week when they're on vacation or sick, some stranger shows up to host. You might consider building a regular rotation for this role. There may be one primary host and small group of secondary hosts in the rotation. Each host will bring his or her own personality to the role, but it is worth developing a standard set of practices for each to follow. That way things don't vary wildly from week to week.

Worship hosts can make very real connections with worshipers both on-camera and in chat. They can build absolutely authentic relationships when they're willing to engage with worshipers. Andy told me a story about one such relationship that was made between him and a visitor online.

One Sunday morning as the prerecorded worship was premiering online, Andy jumped into chat to welcome everyone. As is his standard practice, he offered a few pleasantries, ending on, "I hope everyone is having a wonderful day."

One of the participants replied, "Nope, not having a wonderful day. It's been a terrible week." Andy replied, "I'm so sorry to hear that, I'd love to pray for you if you'd like. I'm going to private message you my personal Zoom room link, and I'll hang there for 10 minutes after worship. If you'd like to pray, just pop in. If not, no worries. Just know I'm here for you if you need me."

Worship continued, and Andy left his Zoom open. A minute or two after worship, the Zoom doorbell chimed, and Andy let the parishioner in. Andy said, "Hello, friend, how can I pray for you?" The parishioner went on to tell Andy about what had been happening in his life that week. Andy listened intently and then said, "I'm so sorry to hear this. Let me pray for you."

Andy offered up a prayer, and at the conclusion said to his person, "I don't know if I recognize you. Have we met before?" The parishioner said, "Oh no. You wouldn't recognize me. I've never been to your church before. I've only ever worshiped with you online. Thank you for praying for me. You'll be seeing me around."

Now I never asked Andy if this person continued to show up (online or in person) or not, but there's a good bet that after being ministered to in such a personal way, he became a regular.

When it comes to being available to worshipers not just on camera, but in chat, I believe an in-person connection is a great way to build relationships too. Hopefully this pandemic has helped some people transition from online to in-person worshipers.

If a person has only ever worshiped with us online and they come to the physical building, it would be great for them to see that familiar face they've come to know over the course of their online relationship with the church. The man who needed prayer would be thrilled to see Andy's face when he walked in the door.

Above all, relationships are what grow the church --relationships with Jesus and relationships with each other. It's easy to have an "outta sight, outta mind" mentality about those not worshiping with us in the building, but they matter too, and we should strive to build lasting relationships with them as well.

In the next chapter, we'll talk about Real Time Both/And worship. We'll revisit some of these ideas but with a different strategy in mind.

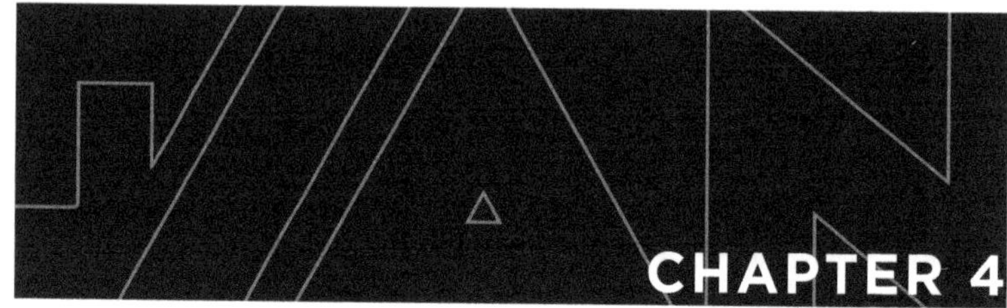

CHAPTER 4 REAL TIME BOTH/AND WORSHIP

"There's no time like the present. No present like time."

-Georgia Byng

When most people think about streaming worship, they often think first about livestreaming. Livestreaming is exactly what it sounds like --streaming what's happening in the moment in real time online. In the first days of the pandemic shutdown, many churches rushed to get online in any way they could. While the early adopters were already there, the newcomers scrambled to find a way to bring worship to their congregations who were all sheltering in place at home. Many used the technology they already had at their disposal, their smartphones, tablets, and computers, and most were streaming worship in real time on Facebook or YouTube. It wasn't until the initial dust settled from being forced online that people realized they could prerecord or even post-edit their worship experiences.

WHAT IS REAL TIME BOTH/AND WORSHIP?

In this chapter we will explore what I call "Real Time Both/And Worship." While I can understand why every church would want to employ this approach, I don't think it's the best solution for everyone. To do it well in a Both/And way takes some real work and intentional strategies. There are a ton of upside advantages to Real Time Both/And worship but also huge potential to lose many of the gains we've made during the pandemic.

I define Real Time Both/And worship as worship that is designed in such a way that attention is given to multiple audiences simultaneously. This happens live "in the moment" and may include a combination of live and prerecorded elements.

There are upsides and downsides to this model. Let's start with the upsides.

1) YOUR ENTIRE CHURCH CAN WORSHIP TOGETHER AT THE SAME TIME

This is one of my favorite upsides. While some will elect to watch later on demand, you have an option where people gathered in the physical space and those worshiping in the digital space can all worship together at the same time. This allows you to think of your entire congregation at the same time. They are just worshiping from different locations.

2) REAL TIME ENGAGEMENT IS POSSIBLE

With this strategy, you have more opportunities for participation and real time engagement. You can conduct polls, receive prayer requests, take questions, chat, share reflections, and so much more. Platforms like Altar (altarlive.com) and Church Online Platform (https://open.life.church) allow you to take the experience to a whole other level with real time chat, prayer, participant video, and more. Your people can even help you shape the narrative as worship is happening.

3) KILL MULTIPLE BIRDS WITH ONE STONE

With real time Both/And worship, you don't have to come in ahead of time and record everything, then edit, upload, and turn around and do it again live. While you may prerecord some elements, you'll do the bulk of the worship live in the moment. This will allow you to serve multiple audiences at the same time. You don't have to double up with this strategy.

4) KEEP YOUR CONGREGATION IN SYNC

If you're trying to keep your worshiping community on more-or-less the same schedule, this one has the most potential to do that. Asynchronous worship is here to stay since people can watch on demand, but this strategy gives you the best shot at keeping everyone together. This particular upside will make even more sense when we get to Post Both/And worship. In that approach, release of the service online may be intentionally delayed.

5) YOU CAN ENGAGE MULTIPLE AUDIENCES AT ONE TIME

There are four distinct audiences we have the opportunity to reach with Real Time Both/And Worship; we'll break those down a little later. But whereas the other strategies can reach these audiences separately, Real Time Both/And worship gives you the opportunity to reach more people at the same time.

There are some downsides to this kind of synchronous worship too:

1) YOUR ATTENTION IS SPLIT

While it's entirely possible to do so, it is very challenging to equally give your attention to people both in the room and online at the same time. In a Both/And scenario, you now have to preach to the left side of the room, to the center of the room, to the right side of the room, to the balcony (if you have one of those), and to the camera where a significant portion of your congregation is sitting.

2) MORE PEOPLE ARE NEEDED TO PULL IT OFF

You may have to have more people involved on the production side with this model. Someone has to monitor the stream. Someone has to run the camera or cameras. And someone has to handle the chat. If you are including graphics, this might require yet another team member. I have seen churches put all of this on one person's shoulders with livestreaming. I would not recommend that because it's too many things to monitor at once.

3) TIME IS A PROBLEM

You have to deal with the time factor. Most of the churches I've spoken to in 2020/2021 have told me that their worship is around an hour, or a little over. Nona Jones suggests under 40 minutes. How can you do that in real time? I'll give you two solutions to consider further ahead.

4) WE MAY REVERT TO THE OLD WAY

The biggest downside and the one that concerns me most is that many churches choosing the real time approach will revert to the pre-pandemic model. They'll talk to the room and forget the online audience is there. Since we can't see them, they don't count.

5) IT'S COMPLICATED

This is by far the most complicated form of planning to do if you're going to do it in a truly hybrid way. You have to think about multiple audiences at once.

KEY CONSIDERATIONS FOR REAL TIME BOTH/AND WORSHIP

Real time Both/And worship may be the most challenging form of Both/And to pull off, but it's also the most rewarding. If I could wave a magic wand and grant the technology, willingness, and ability to every church I work with to do it, this would be the approach that every church would take. Unfortunately, without really meaning to, many churches create a livestreaming service that turns their congregation into spectators or observers of an experience they're not really a part of anymore.

When I was first approached about creating a training on the topic of hybrid worship, I thought long and hard about how I could help people see what a truly hybrid experience looked like. The metaphor of translating stories from "book to film" mentioned before was an extremely helpful tool in helping me frame the concepts in my first training on exclusively online worship. I needed something that tangible for hybrid worship.

The first Both/And trainings were scheduled for mid-November 2020. One Monday night in September I turned on an NFL football game. That's when it hit me! Professional live sporting events are Both/And experiences. Whether you attend the game and sit amongst the fans in the stadium or you watch with friends from your couch, you're taking in a hybrid experience.

There are advantages and disadvantages to both forms of participation. At the game, the energy of the crowd enhances the experience of the game. You can participate in the wave, yell along with the crowd as they chant, and boo and cheer in unison when you like or hate a call that's been made. The sights and sounds, from the "Jumbotron" (Do they still call it that?) to the t-shirt cannon, make you feel something that isn't at all captured in the home. The smell of beer and hot dogs fills the air as vendors bark out "cold beer here," yet another classic Americana moment that doesn't translate to the broadcast version of the game. At home you have closeups and instant replay. Graphics are projected on the field to tell you where the line of scrimmage is. You always know how far a team has to go to achieve a first down or touchdown, and the score/clock is always on the screen awaiting your glance. At home, you have much more comfortable seating, cheaper snacks, and (I hope) less disgusting restrooms. If you have bad seats at the stadium, an argument could be made that watching at home is a better experience. Also keep in mind that not everything at the stadium translates to "at home." For instance, if a player gets injured during a game, things stop. At home, the television producers will show a pre-produced highlight reel and scores from other games, and commentators will talk to the broadcast audience in hopes that you don't turn the channel. At the stadium, you watch the golf cart drive out, the medical team tend to the player, and if it's bad enough, you watch them drive the player off the field. Everyone who works at the stadium, from the vendors to the ushers, are there to give you a great experience. You are their primary concern. They're not thinking a whole lot about the people watching at home. The people who run the cameras, the producers, those responsible for graphics in the production booth, are completely focused on capturing the game for those not in the stadium. They want to keep the folks at home engaged. The people in the stadium are not their primary concern. They are mere scenery, providing the occasional cutaway from time to time. Both models offer an exciting and hopefully riveting experience. They happen at the same time, but the preparation for and attention to each is significantly different.

How can we begin to think of worship in a similar way? Worship that is happening in real time can be captured in a Both/And way where both kinds of attenders think of themselves as the primary audience. In order to pull that off, we have to make some intentional choices. Failure to do so will mean we'll always default to the room.

I recently conducted a poll at a live event that was being offered in a hybrid way. Those registered had expressed interest in doing Both/And worship at their churches. The poll offered four options for respondents to choose from. Each indicated where attention was to be focused in worship.

Here were the options:

A. Our priority is on the people in the room. We stream, but our focus is really on creating an experience for people in the room.

B. We intentionally create an experience for people both in the room and online. We've adapted our practices in worship so people at home and in person feel like they're an equal priority.

C. Our online audience is our priority. We're happy to have people gather in person, but we've streamlined everything so that people at home are fully engaged.

D. We're doing an all-digital service. We don't have anyone in the room when we stream. We're 100% focused on those participating online.

If you had to answer that poll today, which choice would you make?

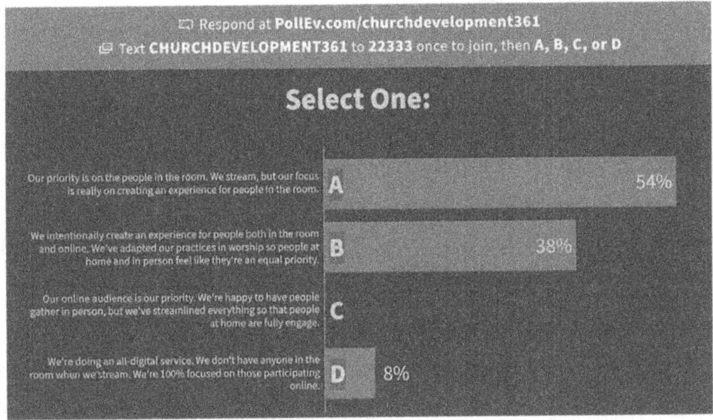

I was a little disappointed at the results. Almost 55% of those who responded were in the A category. About 38% were living into B. When I conducted the same poll on Facebook, the numbers were slightly better for option B at 48% vs. 43% for A.

While I believe every church is likely to want to be in category B, without some real intentional effort and strategy, most will land in A. We can see the people in category A with our physical eyes, so it's easy to give them the most attention. I'm hoping that since you picked up this book, you're working towards category B, and I hope you get there. It makes all the difference for everyone involved.

Monologue to Dialogue

My favorite thing about Both/And worship, especially Real Time Both/And worship, is that it has allowed us to move from monologue to dialogue with our congregations.

Pre-pandemic, worship was more like a traditional broadcast model. We basically had one-way communication in worship. It was from stage (or chancel) to people. Outside of the African American tradition of call and response where participation is encouraged and often expected, many churches have never incorporated much participation into the experience. Interaction was largely limited to responsive prayers, the sharing of prayer requests, "joys and concerns," and "Spirit sightings." In other words, our worship was pretty one-sided, leader to people, and not much the other way around. Because we have now have chat, Zoom, texting, and other means to interact at our disposal, we have the ability to dialogue in worship. These opportunities are dramatically increased with the real time Both/And strategy.

My friend Pastor Kelly McCuaig in Alamogordo, New Mexico has really leaned into the practice of creating a dialogue with his congregation in hybrid worship. I've had the honor of coaching this medium-sized United Methodist Church throughout 2020 and 2021. Grace Church first went online when the pandemic began, and they're doing a tremendous job of iterating and innovating. Here are two examples from Grace Church that demonstrate what's possible where dialogue is concerned:

1) DIGITAL GREETING (OR "PASSING THE PEACE")

One of the most frequently "borrowed" practices participants in my webinar rave about is what I've come to call the digital greeting or passing of the peace. This was Kelly's brain-child and it goes a little something like this:

"Friends, we're so glad to be gathered this morning for worship both here in the building and online. For those of you here in person, I'm going to ask you to do something we didn't used to do in worship. Take out your phones. Mute them, and navigate to our Facebook livestream. For those of you online, you're already one step ahead of us – that's how you're seeing us right now. Navigate to the chat and take a moment to greet one another right now. Let us pass the peace of Christ in these moments from wherever we are worshiping from."

You could use a QR code in print form or on the screen to help people navigate to your Facebook or YouTube page quickly. As you familiarize your congregation with this ritual, it will become easier and easier as you go. The beauty of this dialogue is that it allows everyone to participate regardless of where they're worshiping from. It also eliminates a lot of the physical contact that used to be associated with this time in worship.

2) REAL TIME REFLECTIONS AND QUESTIONS

The second example I share, which isn't something Kelly does all the time, but is also a favorite of attendees, is a clip from a series he did entitled "Questions for God." The service begins with Kelly inviting people both in person and at home to submit their questions in real time. These questions will play a large role in the sermon he'll deliver a little later.

Kelly gives instructions in such a way that favors neither the room nor those online. Everyone is an equal participant. He explains that worshipers can submit their questions via text, via chat, or they can write their questions on a slip of paper and hand them in to an usher who is coming through the aisles.

The middle portion of worship is edited out in this clip, and then after a fade up from black, we see Kelly come forward and say, "Ok, now for the fun part. These just got submitted to me. We're going to rapid fire these questions." He begins artfully working his way through the questions one by one. Some were submitted by people in person. Others were submitted by people worshiping online.

What I love so much about this example is that everyone has the opportunity to participate in the service. The congregation – worshiping from multiple locations – is helping to shape the content in the service. There's nothing like hearing your pastor read your question or reflection and respond to it to make you feel like you're a part of what's happening in real time. It's truly a dialogue when leaders engage participants in the moment.

Dialogues move people from watchers of worship to worshipers online, and from viewers to participants. When we do that, we create moments of worship that transcend the space we're worshiping in and the technology that's making it possible.

Transcendence

How do you know you've created a transcendent expression of worship both online and in the building? Worship where the technology disappears and people are moved to deeper personal faith, an "all in" mentality, in which they want to change the world through mission? If you look carefully, you can see it in the way your people are engaging with worship inside and outside of it.

My friend Rev. George Ashford pastors a largely African American church in Columbia, South Carolina. Journey Church is part of the United Methodist denomination, worshiping at 650 before the pandemic hit. This is a large church by UMC standards.

George and his team are doing incredible things with Both/And worship. They are ahead of the curve with when it comes to streaming, capturing their worship experience with a three-camera setup, graphics, and professional lighting. Large LED panels are nestled behind the preacher, providing an inspiring backdrop for even more inspired preaching. You'll find QR codes throughout the building for easy scanning of would-be print pieces, advertising activities happening in the life of the church.

Like every church, Journey Church had to shut their worship down when Covid reared its ugly head. George shifted strategies and developed worship with more intentionality on how people at home were experiencing it by framing shots more tightly, putting the numbers up on the screen for those who were worshiping online (so those in the in-person crowd could be aware of them), inviting the in-person attenders to wave to those worshiping at home, calling out by name those who texted, and projecting Facebook chat and reading comments live during worship. His team also created what he calls the "Amen Section."

In the Amen Section, three high-top tables sit off to the left of the stage where team members (called Social Media Ambassadors) monitor chat, greet worshipers online, and care for them through digital means as worship is happening live. From time to time, they actually give voice to the digital congregation by shouting out select comments in the chat. When someone types out, "Preach it Brother Ashford," a Social Media Ambassador may actually yell that comment out on behalf of the person who posted it. Over the course of the hour, 774 comments were posted in the chat. The people were engaged! This is what the move from monologue to dialogue is all about.

Behind the Amen Section is a large whiteboard. On it, among other things, the team writes the number of people worshiping online in real time. As I watched the board throughout the morning, the number grew from 30, to 50, to 75, and it continued to increase until it was up over 120.

This is done not only so Pastor Ashford can see how many are participating online. It also is meant for the people in the room – to keep them aware of those they can't see with their eyes.

The return to in-person worship has only brought about 20% of Journey's faith community back to the building; 80% of this congregation is still worshiping from home.

What's fascinating is that giving has gone up in this season, and I'm told by George and associate pastor Marty Quick that engagement in small groups, Bible study, and missional activity has also increased in the year and a half that has transpired since the pandemic began. How do you know you've created hybrid worship that transcends the physical building? People at home aren't just spectators; they're participants. They're involved in the conversation as its happening. They help shape the content.

When I visited George for a secret worshiper consultation in August of 2021, there was a moment where George sat his phone on the pulpit in front of him and proclaimed that he was going to take a look at the chat and see what people were saying. Within a few seconds he began to read out some of the comments, one of which he lingered on for a moment. He began to respond to a woman in his church who was going through a particularly difficult time in her life. He began to lift that woman up, quoted some scripture and followed The Spirit's lead, preaching for a moment and addressing her very needs. Her participation helped shape the content.

The result of transcendence also reveals itself in how people participate with their pocketbooks, and how they continue to show up in the building and online. Journey Church has seen increased giving and missional participation. Bible studies online far surpass what was happening in the building pre-pandemic, and people are more engaged in missional activities than ever before.

George is so bought in to Both/And that he told me he now considers Journey Church an online church with an in-person option. This has helped him reframe his thinking about how important it is to connect with the people not physically present.

Dealing with Time

When it comes to Real Time Both/And worship, there are several challenges we have to sort through. The first is how to do deal with the time challenges of shorter online worship while offering a longer in-person experience.

We've established that shorter is better when it comes to online worship. People who worship in-person come with an excitement and expectation for something that is often an hour or more. Online, 40 minutes is the recommended threshold. How can you do both of those things in real time?

Here are two options for how to consolidate:

OPTION 1: SPLIT THE DIFFERENCE

I'll be honest in saying I'm not super fond of this one, but it's an option some churches are using and finding success with. If an hour in person is what you did pre-pandemic or that's where you'd like to be now and 40 minutes is the maximum recommended length for online worship, you might just compromise with a 50-minute service. You're basically just splitting the difference between the two times and meeting in the middle.

The downside to this option, and the reason it's not my favorite, is that when everyone compromises, well, everyone compromises. Compromise is hard, and people often don't like to compromise. It's like blended worship. Some churches don't want to make a choice between traditional and contemporary worship styles, so they choose to blend the two together. In almost twenty-five years of coaching, I've seen very few successful models for blended worship. You've got one segment of your worshiping congregation who loves hymns and another segment that loves drums and guitar. The problem is those hymn lovers often hate drums and guitar, and the drums and guitar people aren't very fond of hymns. So, what do we do? We do hymns with drums and guitar - giving everyone something to hate in the same service. In an attempt to be all things to all people, we end up being nothing to no one. Compromising your worship service to a shorter length might make it so neither group – not the people in the room, nor the people online - are very happy about the split-the-difference length.

The people who show up for in-person – the ones who had been worshiping in their pajamas with coffee in their hands (the coffee they aren't allowed to bring into your worship space) - don't want to be cheated out of 10 minutes of that in-person experience. After all, they actually got up and did their hair and makeup. They made the extra effort to drive in and don't want you to cut it short. When it comes to the people online, they won't complain if you go past 40 minutes. They'll just turn it off if it feels like it's gone on too long. I don't love this model, but it's working for some people, and I'd never discount someone's positive experience.

OPTION 2: THE STAGGERED APPROACH

The second option is what I call the staggered approach. The idea is that you start your in-person first, with your focus solely on those gathered in person. Ten to fifteen minutes later you begin the worship stream inviting those worshiping online into the live experience. What you're essentially doing is cutting out the singing or some of the other elements that people may not be heavily participating in from home anyway. For example, a worship host, pastor, or leader might welcome everyone in the room at 10 AM to worship. That same leader or another leader would kick off worship with a prelude or opening piece of music, then offer a spoken word recap of the present series or set up the topic for the day. That leader might then invite those in the building to engage in the singing portion of worship. As all of this is offered, the leader is only addressing and thinking about the people in the room. There is no one online yet. The stream hasn't begun.

Let's say in this scenario the worship leader is going to sing five songs. The in-person crowd would sing three or four of those songs and then after song three or four the livestream would begin. The worship host, liturgist, pastor, or another leader would then welcome the online audience with the same (or an abbreviated) spoken piece to catch them up to where they are in the series or for that particular day. There are three possibilities for how the online congregation would be welcomed in:

1) Possibility one

The same person who welcomed the congregation in the room would welcome the online audience once the stream starts. This would happen in front of the people in the room, so it would be a little redundant, but I believe those present would accept this practice and get used to it in no time. The leader would address the camera and offer words of welcome to those gathered online with the theme setup or recap playing out just as it had before. That leader would then invite the online audience to sing the final song or two along with the in-person gathering. These would be the only songs the online audience would sing.

2) Possibility two

Instead of the people in the room hearing the same intro twice, you might consider prerecording the welcome for the online crowd. While it requires a bit more technical expertise and third-party software, there are multiple advantages to this possibility.

First, the in-person crowd won't have to hear the intro and setup a second time for the online crowd. When you finish singing that third or fourth song, the music leader will invite the congregation to pray. When that prayer begins, the go live button is pressed and once live, the prerecorded intro video is played. While this is happening, the music leader is praying with one eye open waiting for a cue from the back of the room to move on to the final songs.

The second advantage is that you know exactly how long the welcome will be for the online congregation. This allows everyone to plan accordingly. The worship host can offer a self-intro, welcome, recap, or theme setup and then invite the online congregation to continue with worship in song.

From the back of the room, the media team will count down – five, four, three, two, one, and then the music leader will begin song number four or five bringing the online audience in sync with the in-person audience.

3) Possibility three

The most technically complex possibility, but the one with the most potential for connection, involves a live worship host talking to the camera in real time from another room. Using wireless technology, a camera or even a smartphone might be taken into another room in the building, where the host can do all of the aforementioned things live in the moment. The advantage here is that they can call people out by name in real time, mention specific comments in the chat, and can vamp as long as needed while other things are happening in the room. This possibility might also allow you to time things in such a way that you aren't relying on the prayer to be a transition, but the welcome could come as the third or fourth song is being played. To recap, with this model, you're going to cut ten to fifteen minutes off the beginning of the service for the online congregation. You're doing this by starting the livestream after some of the songs (and other things) have been done in person. By staggering the online start time and inviting the online audience to participate in the last song or two, they'll have a shorter version of the music portion of worship.

The middle part of the service can be mostly in sync, although we'll explore some alternative things you might do for the online audience in a bit. Just be sure to look at the camera from time to time, and also remember that the audience may tune in on delay.

After the sermon – if you've taken my advice to move the announcements to the end and make them actions steps – you could instead say something like, "We're a church that lives into this [insert connection about today's topic] in many ways. You can find all of the latest opportunities to live this out by visiting us at: www.nameofyourchurch.com/whatshappeningnow.com." This not only shaves time off the service, saving you three or four minutes of announcements because you're not sharing every announcement, it also makes those announcements evergreen.

Remember that even one week after the camp bake sale announcement is given, that info is useless. If an online viewer watches six months later and you introduce them to a current events page and tie it to your topic, they can get involved at that moment rather than experience a bunch of outdated information. From there, you might also cut out the song or songs of response at the end, saving another four or five minutes.

So, putting it all together, after the sermon, you might say something like this, "Friends, we are a church that is finding our faith in the midst of fear in many ways. You can learn about how you can find your faith and live it out by visiting our website [insert url]. For those of you worshiping with us online, we hope you'll consider being a part of what we're doing all throughout the week. Thanks for joining us for worship, and we hope to see you again next week at 10 AM here in the building, or online at 10:15. Have a great rest of the week." In the room, you'd continue by singing your song or songs of response and anything else you might typically do after that. Your online stream can come to its completion at that time. This ending can be done using one of the three possibilities outlined above.

If the person that welcomed the in-person gathering offers these closing words, those in the room will be aware of the dismissal of the online congregation, as they'll hear those words spoken in real time. If you prerecord this closing, the people in the room will be unaware of that dismissal. It's slightly less cumbersome and disruptive to their experience of worship. Finally, if you're doing this from another room in real time, the people in the room are unaware of it, and you have the advantage of engaging with people in a more organic way.

With all of these possibilities at your disposal, creating a staggered real-time worship becomes an exciting opportunity. Basically, you're effectively creating a one-hour (more or less) live experience with a 35 – 40-minute online experience pocketed within it.

If you'd like all of the upsides of engaging with your congregation in real time but want to have service times that fit each respective group (in-person, online, and on delay) the staggered approach may be the best for you.

Not Everything in the Room Translates to Online

At this point in the book, we've pretty much established that the experience in the building is very different than the experience online. It's worth mentioning again however that we must think differently about how what we do is received by those participating from different places in different times. Failure to do so dishonors those who are or may eventually become part of our community.

During a recent sermon, a pastor I coach in North Carolina named Rev. Marilyn Weiler (Pine Grove UMC) addressed the nature of participating in different places at difference times and what it means to our congregations. She used such beautiful language during her sermon, which described the intentionality we should bring to everyone's experience of worship. She said, "My friends, our unity as God's people causes us to celebrate and value extravagant hospitality. It calls us to create a place where we are connected to one another, whether in-person or via the internet. It is a place of respect, acceptance, and friendship. It offers attentive listening and mutual sharing of lives and life stories." She goes on to acknowledge the extreme challenge that the shift to hybrid worship has been for her church in the wake of Covid-19, boldly declaring the intentionality the church must bring to worship and ministry in the post-pandemic era. Marilyn encourages her congregation to really "see one another," so that they can "extend respect and lift one another up with dignity."[1]

Having dignity and respect for your congregation means that you don't favor one audience over the others. It means we don't rank people in terms

1. Pine Grove UMC Worship: The Tie That Binds – Anointed, Week 6, July 4, 2021, https://www.youtube.com/watch?v=CM5lFvayTRM.

of their importance by where they sit. The people in the front of the room are not more important than the people in the back of the room. The people in the back are not more important than the people who sit in the balcony and overflow spaces. And all of those people are not more important than the people who are worshiping from their living rooms, hotel rooms, vacation, or wherever they may be sitting. They are all our congregation, regardless of where they sit.

You may be thinking, "That's unfair. We don't rank people by where they sit." Let me suggest to you that your language may be giving you away. Our instructions often favor the room. They also favor the people who are participating in real time. We often don't think enough about the person watching on delay. We mustn't allow our language to give us away – that we're only thinking about the people we can physically see with our eyes. Let's show them all dignity and respect with our language.

DEVELOPING BOTH/AND LANGUAGE

Without meaning to, we really favor the in-person segment of our congregation with our language. I've been working my way through about 60 secret worshiper consultations over the last month, and I've lost count of how many times I've heard leaders say, "let's stand together and worship," or "let's stand together for the reading of the scripture." Do we really believe that people at home watching on their smart TVs or on their cell phones are going to stand up for either of those things? Probably not. This language tips them off to the fact that we really aren't thinking much about them.

What if we instead used Both/And language to encourage engagement from multiple audiences? We could instead say "If you're worshiping with us here in-person, I'd like to invite you to stand and sing and if you're worshiping with us online, I'd invite you to find a posture that would allow you to fully participate in these moments." That inclusive language shows dignity and respect to your online audience.

Just a few weeks ago I was worshiping at home with my family in our living room, participating in an online worship service. The pastor at this service innocently said – not looking at the camera I might add – "If you'd like to pray with someone today, you can find one of our care pastors in the back of the room. They'd be happy to pray with you." I turned to my wife and jokingly said, "Well, honey, I guess I'm going to have to change out of my PJs, jump in the car, and drive over to the church, because I want to pray with someone."

Language matters, and the language that was used in that moment could be perceived as an indicator that I and others who are participating online aren't really being considered. What made this more frustrating for me is that there are servants at this church who monitor the chat and will pray with an online participant if they'd like to pray – even in real time.

I don't fault this pastor for the unintentional language; it wasn't malicious. We all have to work on our language. Even as I'm teaching, I find myself saying "watching worship" rather than "worshiping online." It's a hard habit to break, but one I'm committed to overcoming.

A mindset shift – that our entire congregation matters regardless of where they sit - will be reflected in our language. The moment described above could very well have been said in a Both/And way: "If you're worshiping with us in-person and you'd like to pray with someone, you can find a care pastor in the back of the room. If you're worshiping online with us in real time, one of our digital care pastors would be happy to pray with you in the chat, and finally - and don't forget about these folks – if you're worshiping with us later and you'd like to pray with someone, drop us an email at [insert email address] and we'll be happy to pray with you."

When it comes to participatory moments, we can very easily forget the people not in the room. I've heard on numerous occasions references to the bulletin or things that might be picked up on the way into the room, with no option available to those gathered online. Communion is especially tricky. Be really careful with your language here and remember that the people online and even on delay still may want to be a part of this holy moment.

In one service I attended online, the pastor (who up until this point had done pretty well with Both/And language) said, "You all received a little communion packet when you came in the room. Go ahead and take that out and lift the film on the top exposing the bread…" No… No pastor, I didn't get one of those when I came into my living room and turned on the TV. So how can I participate? Is that possible?[2]

2. I know there are some big theological questions people are wrestling with where communion is concerned. I'm going to assume you've wrestled through those or will do so as you're developing your Both/And rites and rituals. I try to refrain from making blanket statements about what you should do with communion because there is such diverse thinking about this sacrament.

Whether you pre-bless elements and allow people to pick them up at your church ahead of time, bless them over the world wide web, substitute a "love feast" for communion, or just tell people to use what they have, be mindful that the people at home need intentional language too.

Many readers of this book believe the communion table is open to anyone, and if we want our Both/And communion to reflect that, we've got be intentional about truly opening it up for worshipers participating in different ways.

Finally, be mindful of your language for an audience watching on delay. We are sometimes in the habit of saying things like, "Good morning, I hope you're having a great Sunday," as we open up worship. While that is perfect for the people in the room and online watching in real time, it creates a slight disconnect for those worshiping on delay. It is very possible that someone will be watching your service later in the week - maybe during their lunch break at work or when they have a free moment at home. If they happen to be watching on Tuesday afternoon, the "morning" and "Sunday" language creates a slight disconnect. Better language might be something more like, "Welcome to worship, we hope you're having a great day." The little language shift there opens things up a bit.

I'm not suggesting you wear avoiding temporal language like handcuffs, but why not make it as inclusive as possible? I don't think you can lose anything by saying "good morning" or mentioning the day of the week, but I do believe you can gain something by using inclusive language instead. After all, inclusive language extends to every segment of your congregation. In time, with practice, it will all become second nature.

KEEPING ONLINE WORSHIPERS ENGAGED

Alternate Moments

Since not everything translates to the online audience, we might consider having two different tracks for certain moments in worship. Some moments that work so well in the room become very much a moment of disconnect for the people participating at home. Moments where the online congregation can't see what's happening or they're not invited in can prompt them to reach for the remote or click the close window button pretty fast. Alternate moments are moments that the in-person audience will not see, but people worshiping at home will appreciate and keep them engaged. They might include a video, an interactive moment, engagement by a live host, or anything else that makes the in-person audience feel connected.

Returning to our original football game metaphor for a moment: an alternate moment is a little like what happens when there is a player injured or there is some other kind of delay. The producers, camera operators, and engineers in the booth would never just focus the camera on an injured player and leave the shot on for the entire duration that that player is being tended to. Instead, they are going to cut to a pre-produced highlights reel from earlier in the season. Or they might cut to the scores of other games. The commentators are going to banter back and forth to keep you engaged. Basically, they're going to do whatever they can to keep you from changing the channel.

So, what can an alternate moment look like? Here are a couple options:

PRE-PRODUCED VIDEO

Recently I visited a church that did a backpack collection/blessing to prepare kids for going back to school. This church partnered with congregants and local organizations to fill each bag with all of the supplies needed to start the year off right. On the week I was visiting them, over one hundred backpacks were brought forward to be prayed over before being sent on their way to the foster kids who would benefit from them. This was a relatively small church, so seeing this huge response was inspiring.

As backpack after backpack came forward, there was a healthy pride felt by the members of this congregation for this great work that was playing out before us. I snapped photos, and from my vantage point I could clearly see everything that was taking place. After worship, I reviewed the archived livestream and I realized just how different this experience was for the online audience. This church had a single Mevo camera on a stand near the back of the room. It did an adequate job of capturing worship, although I'd love to have seen it be a little closer.

Watching the stream gave me a very different impression of this moment. At one point as people were bringing the backpacks up, people were standing directly in front of the camera. For much longer than was comfortable, I saw someone's backside. The line was long, and people were staying socially distanced, so it took quite a while for this to play out.

What you couldn't see from the camera's vantage point was the front of the room where the backpacks were being collected. Quite frankly, it was a mess on camera. That afternoon I looked on the church's website to learn more about the backpack giveaway. I learned more about some of the organizations they worked with. I also found an excellently produced video that had been used to tell the story of the backpack weekend on social media. In the video I saw shots of smiling kids receiving their gear, heard from program directors, volunteers, and school representatives about how meaningful this program was. It was all very inspiring. The video was a little over three minutes long, and as I timed out the moment in worship, I discovered that it took a little over three minutes for the backpacks to come forward. When I went back to the team to share my observations, I suggested that a better way to keep people at home engaged during those kinds of moments was to play a pre-produced piece like the one they already had at their disposal. It was an ah-ha moment for all of us.

An alternate moment might have looked like this:

"Friends, this morning is our blessing of the backpacks collection weekend. We have over one hundred bags coming forward this morning that have been purchased, stuffed, and prayed over by the people of our church. If you've got a bag to bring forward, I'm going to invite you to do that in a moment. If you're worshiping with us online today, here is what the blessing of the backpacks is all about."

The media team would then roll the video that would play only for the online audience. The video doesn't need to be shown in the room. What's playing out live in the moment is more inspiring than the video. Seeing those backpacks come up is moving.

As the video is nearing its completion, someone from the booth would then count down with their fingers in the air from five down to one, letting the pastor or leader know the video is almost over. The pastor or leader might then say right on cue (and as the video has completed), "Let us pray over these backpacks and the children who will carry them throughout this school year." From that moment on, the room and online is back in sync. The alternate moment becomes a seamless engagement that works in a Both/And way.

LIVE INTERACTION - BREAKING THE FOURTH WALL

Another way that you might engage the online audience with an alternate moment is to talk directly to those at home in real time while the room is doing something else. When things are happening in the room that don't translate, there's no reason you can't have someone on camera talk directly to the audience participating at home without addressing the room. My friend Rev. Ben Gosden, pastor of Trinity United Methodist Church in Savannah, Georgia, calls this "breaking the fourth wall," and it's become a regular practice in his worship services.

Many of us are familiar with the concept of breaking the fourth wall as it pertains to film and television. TVtropes.org defines breaking the fourth wall like this:

> Breaking the fourth wall is when a character acknowledges their fictionality, by either indirectly or directly addressing the audience. Alternatively, they may interact with their creator (the author of the book, the director of the movie, the artist of the comic book, etc.). This is more akin to breaking one of the walls of the set, but the existence of a director implies the existence of an audience, so it's still indirectly Breaking The Fourth Wall. This trope is usually used for comedic purposes.[3]

If you've ever seen the film *Ferris Bueller's Day Off*, the titular character in the film, Ferris Bueller, regularly breaks the fourth wall to talk to the audience. The same is true for the campy, but totally awesome 80s/90s sitcom *Saved by the Bell*, where lead character Zack Morris regularly calls a "timeout" and talks directly to the audience.

At Trinity, Ben does Real Time Both/And worship. He tells me that when he's offering the communion liturgy (setup) the mic is on in the house speakers, and when he's finished inviting people to come forward to receive communion, they turn off the sound system in the room and leave on the mic for online. He will then talk directly to the audience gathered online by looking directly at the camera. This could include many different conversations ranging from how to participate in communion from home, to what communion means and why we do it, to telling the story of his own first communion.

As Ben is talking to the people online, he can monitor what's happening in the space as communion servers are tending to the congregation. Once they're finished, the sound system in the room is turned back on, and then he prays, bringing the room back into sync with the online audience.

3. "Breaking the Fourth Wall," TVTropes, accessed September 23, 2021, https://tvtropes.org/pmwiki/pmwiki.php/Main/BreakingTheFourthWall.

Ben tells me this has worked wonderfully for his entire congregation as they worship from multiple locations.

MELDING MULTIPLE AUDIENCES INTO ONE CONGREGATION

In my Both/And trainings, I sometimes see discomfort expressed when I use the word audience to describe engagement with those worshiping in-person and online. As I see it, we have one congregation that is made up of different audiences. I'd prefer not to think of them as different congregations, but instead one congregation worshiping from different locations.

In this Both/And world, we now have to consider that there are four distinct audiences that make up our congregation. Creating moments of participation and interaction for all of them is essential in creating Both/And worship.

Let's define those audiences, and then we'll look at how to engage or meld them together.

1) THE IN-PERSON AUDIENCE

These are the people we can see with our eyes. They're the ones who have shown up in the building. They usually get most of our attention. After all, we can see their heads nodding, can hear their voices, see the smiles on their faces, and experience their reactions in real time. Without intentionally making a choice, these folks will always be the ones we favor.

2) THE AT HOME BUT CONNECTED TO YOUR FAITH COMMUNITY AUDIENCE

You know these folks. They haven't come back to the building yet, or maybe they have and they're away on vacation, are snowbirds, or aren't physically present for some other reason. At one point in time, they were regular worshipers in the building. Some of them are probably members, givers, and involved in your church. Of all the people who join us online, these are the ones we think about most because we have actual relationships with them.

3) THE VISITOR/GUEST NOT CONNECTED TO YOUR FAITH COMMUNITY AUDIENCE

These people probably don't count as part of your congregation yet. You don't know them. They don't love you yet. They're just checking you out. Maybe they happened upon your Facebook Live link, you came up in a YouTube search, or maybe someone in your congregation shared a link they clicked on.

We often don't give enough thought to these people as we're doing worship, in part because they are a mystery to us. They're a number on an analytics chart that we can't exactly figure out why they came or who they are.

When the pandemic forced many online or changed the strategy for those who were already online, we gained a whole new audience. Some of these folks are people who never would have walked into our buildings but now they're intrigued and seeing what this whole church thing is all about.

Every church should consider how to build bridges into our rituals and practices through orientation language. We should also develop opportunities to connect with them in order to build real relationships. How can we make those guests feel valued and welcomed?

4) THE "THOSE WHO WATCH ON DELAY" AUDIENCE

From the beginning of the pandemic until now and by the time you hold this book in your hands, the number of people who are worshiping on delay is growing exponentially. I think this freaks many of us out. How do we serve an audience who doesn't show up on Sunday and might not watch until later in the week? How do we adapt for binge watchers?

It's not a huge surprise that in a Disney+, Netflix, Amazon Prime Video culture, people would eventually move to a more on-demand model for worship. Rather than panic as we try and figure it out, I believe that if we reimagine worship with this audience in mind new and exciting possibilities will arise.

Powerful expressions of worship are timeless. It doesn't matter if you encounter a transformational message on the day it was preached, or on the day, year, or week after. If the spark is there, it can ignite something within a listener that can set their faith ablaze.

As I mentioned in an earlier chapter, my favorite film of all time is *The Shawshank Redemption*. When the film came out in 1994, it was a box office flop. It wasn't until 1995 that it began to find an audience as the top rented movie of that year. In 1997 it solidified its status as a classic when it began airing on TNT in heavy rotation. It's regularly found now near the top of best films of all time lists all over the internet.

I was not fortunate enough to see it in the theater when it was released and instead saw it for the first time in 1997. It was as moving the day

I watched it as a rental as it was the day it was released in theaters. It continues to be a moving film even decades later.[4] The power of this story isn't hindered by when it was released. Its masterful storytelling is what makes it so great. The same is possible with worship. How can we meld these four audiences into one congregation? We must craft our worship in such a way that we give attention to each of them equally. This happens through Both/And language, eye contact, and interaction. Let's take a look at how we can incorporate participation into the same worship experience while considering all four congregations.

Years ago, I was invited by the Mountain Sky Conference of The United Methodist Church to develop a set of worship resources for Advent in partnership with a dozen or more pastors. In 2020, I reimagined how this series could work with limited in-person gatherings, keeping in mind these four audiences.

In the series, we were inviting participants to consider the true meaning of the Advent season. We called it "Unwrapping Christmas." Each week of the series focused on a different biblical character. Those characters were juxtaposed against some of the typical trappings of the season. For the reimagined version of the series, I proposed having participants write a prayer on week one of the four-week series. Advent begins four Sundays

4. "The Shawshank Redemption: From Box Office Flop to Global Sensation," *The Signal*, July 27, 2021, https://signalscv.com/2021/07/the-shawshank-redemption-from-box-office-flop-to-global-sensation/.

prior to Christmas. Here's how the invitation to participate in that prayer might play out:

AUDIENCE 1 (IN-PERSON):

Each person receives a piece of paper and a pencil or pen either at the door or awaiting them at their seat. Two stations are at-the-ready up front. One has small cardboard boxes on it, the other station has wrapping paper, tape, and bows.

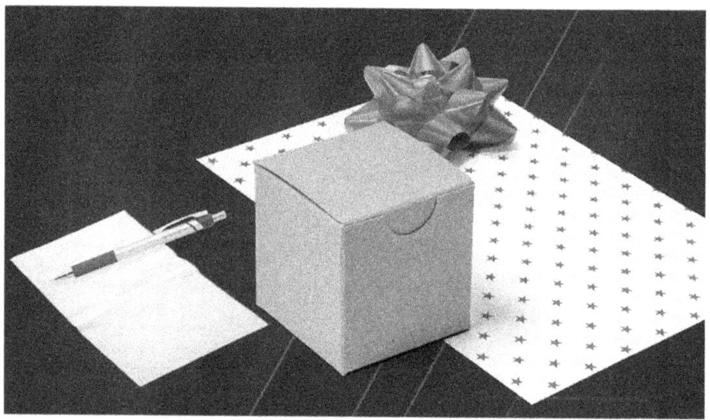

AUDIENCE 2 (AT HOME BUT CONNECTED):

A "send ahead kit" is assembled which includes all the elements described above. A sign-up is advertised in the week(s) prior to the series to give everyone a chance to get one who wants one. A team of volunteers is organized to drive the send ahead kits around town to drop them off at homes. If the budget is large enough to do so, some kits might also be mailed.

AUDIENCE 3 (VISITORS/GUESTS PARTICIPATING FOR THE FIRST TIME):

The pattern to a small cardboard box is created or acquired and uploaded as a PDF file to your website. The same thing is done with wrapping paper. These will be posted in the chat window early in worship, during the first week of the series.

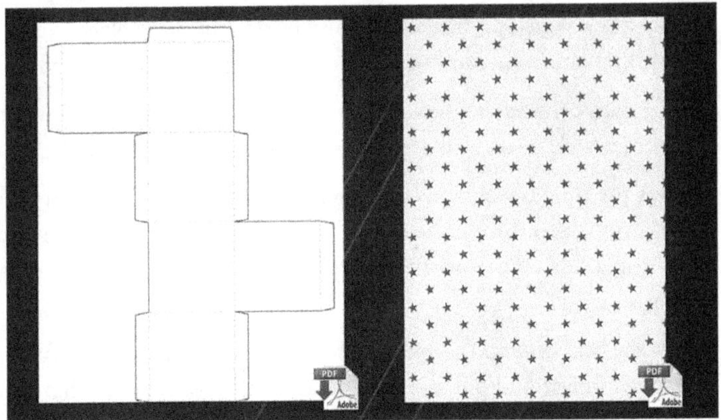

AUDIENCE 4 (THOSE WHO WATCH ON DELAY):

For the people who watch later, you've already created all you need. Post the links to the PDF flies along with your archived service. They go in the description of your video.

THE SCRIPT

Friends, today a little later in the service, we're going to engage in an interactive prayer time. It's week one of Advent and of our Unwrapping Christmas series, and we want to remember all throughout this season why we celebrate Christmas with a special gift-wrapped prayer.

For those of you worshiping here in the room, you received a piece of paper and a pen when you came in. You'll be invited a little later to write a prayer on that paper. At home, some of you received a send ahead kit and you have that same paper and pen.

If you're new with us today or didn't receive a kit, find a piece of paper and something to write with. We'd love for you to participate as well. And if you're watching this at a later time, you might also look for a pen and something to write with. We'd love for you to participate too.

Those in person will be invited to approach the stations up front to put your prayer in a box, then wrap it up. Those with a kit will do the same, and for those of you without a kit, you can find a PDF pattern for a box and a wrapping paper printout in the chat or description of this video.

> Go ahead and print those out now and you can do a little craft project today as we worship. They'll be flimsy boxes, but that's okay. We'll do our prayer later, but you can begin constructing your boxes now.
>
> You'd then continue with worship, giving the people at home time to construct their boxes. Toward the end of worship, you might then say:
>
> Now's the time for our special interactive prayer. Go ahead and write your own prayer, or use the one on the screen, and when you're done put it in a box. When you've finished that wrap it up and put a bow on it.
>
> Now the next time you're in front of your Christmas tree, take that gift-wrapped prayer and put it under the tree along with your other gifts. On Christmas morning unwrap your box and pray that prayer together as you open other presents.
>
> Let's begin now.

What you've essentially done is create a scenario where everyone gets to participate, and no one feels like an afterthought.

Pastor Marylin Weiler of Pine Grove United Methodist Church offered a similar opportunity to her congregation in a recent series called "The Tie That Binds." This series on unity featured the image of cloths being tied together.

As people came into the building, they received strips of cloth to write on. She extended instructions for those online to find a cloth they could write on for later in the service and offered an invite to those watching on delay to participate as well. At the end of her instruction, she let all four audiences know that those strips would be tied together in a bound tapestry residing within the building. She didn't forget to ask people at home to drop their strips off at the church or drop them in the mail so they could all be a part of it too.

REFRAMING THE CAMERA IN WORSHIP

The final aspect of Real Time Both/And worship that many churches face is the resistance people often express about the visibility of the technology in the room. Reframing our thinking is critical in this new era of hybrid worship. Let's face it, to really create an intimate experience of worship for people at home, the camera needs to be close - close enough to capture the leaders from waist to head. Any further back, and online worshipers feel pretty disconnected from the leaders.

In my "Telling the Old Story in a New Time" training I encouraged leaders to follow the Mister Rogers model. In Mister Rogers' Neighborhood, the camera was always pushing in on him as he spoke directly to the camera. While he'd also interact with others on camera, he always remembered the viewers on the other side of it. He also gave viewers time to ponder what he was saying, building in time for reflection. Fred Rogers was a master of making you feel like you were in the room with him. As a child, I felt like I went for a daily visit to his home. Every person involved in the planning, filming, and deployment of worship should brush up on Mister Rogers. Study how the camera moves and how close the shots are. Pay attention to pacing and his interactions with the camera.

As more people have returned to in-person worship, I've seen churches switch their strategy from prerecorded - where everything was up close and personal (intimate) - to going real time where the cameras are moved to the back of the room with the inability to get a real closeup. That shift creates a different experience for the "at home worshiper" accustomed to the intimate nature of prerecorded worship. Wide shots are wonderful for establishing the room and for cutaways, but when a row of singers (be it a choir or a "praise band") are all on the same screen head to toe and you cannot make out facial features, it's very hard to feel connected and invited into the experience. When this happens, we inadvertently turn people at home into watchers or viewers rather than worshipers and participants. We don't consider how far away they feel from us.

Both real time and prerecorded expressions work with an intentional strategy. I'm not suggesting a church has to do one over the other. One advantage to the Pre-Both/And is that you don't have to worry about the camera blocking the congregation when going after that closeup shot in worship

Some people are critical about the presence of technology in our worship spaces. They don't want tripods and cameras present that mar the space up front. They don't like seeing the technology and would rather it be hidden in the back of the room. How quickly we've forgotten that it was only because those cameras were there that we were able to worship during the height of the pandemic. In time, our distraction by the technology fades away. We become less and less aware of it even in the course of one worship service.

A couple of years ago I visited Elevation Church in Charlotte, NC. This megachurch, helmed by Steven Furtick, has been doing hybrid worship for years. They have all the bells and whistles to do it extremely well.

Overhead, in their worship space, they have a giant track with a camera that swoops down over and over throughout the experience. I remember the first time looking up and thinking, "Wow, that's quite the monstrosity." It would run from the back of the room to the front of the auditorium, capturing a very dramatic shot of the sea of people gathered below. It would then retract back to the start of the track and repeat the move again and again.

Ten minutes into the experience, I forgot it was there. What we could see on the screens (IMAG - Image magnification) was so inspiring, the technology faded away. We were focused on worshiping God.

Even if the technology doesn't fade away, is that a bad thing? Could we instead use its presence in the space to help our people recognize the impact our churches are having outside the building?

I've had the incredible opportunity to work with The Western North Carolina Conference of the UMC in a retainer relationship focused on helping churches create intentional Both/And worship experiences. The conference devised a really wonderful two-pronged strategy for this work. They asked me to coach churches on the content side and brought in a friend of mine, streaming guru Chris Carson, to develop some affordable but extremely capable media packages to serve these churches.

Chris created a system that makes use of three Mevo cameras that wirelessly connect to a MacBook Air running on Apple's game changing M1 chip. Each camera sits on a monopod and through the magic of an enterprise level router, it all communicates without having cables strung all over the room. One added benefit is that the cameras can be repositioned at any time. The only real drawback of this system is that the Mevo cameras have no optical zoom. This means that in order to get a closeup, you actually have to position the camera close up. The camera needs to be relatively close to the leaders to get the waist-up shot needed to engage people fully online.

Those of us involved in developing this package anticipated that there might be some pushback from church members who didn't want to have the tripods up front in their sanctuaries. My friend Rob Hutchinson, the Director of Church Development, had a brilliant thought about how to address this challenge. He suggested that we reframe the thinking around what this technology means in the space.

Rob helped me and everyone else see that those tripods and cameras should be celebrated, not lamented. They are a visual representation for those gathered in the room of the reach and impact we're having outside the building. He suggested that we help people recognize that those things aren't just plastic, metal, and glass gizmos ruining the view. Instead, they are a reminder of the people who are worshiping from home, care facilities, jails, vacations, and wherever else people happen to be when worshiping with us online. He also points out that we are not critical of mic stands and other equipment that supports the deployment of worship in the building.

We tend to undervalue vision casting in the church. People resist what they don't understand. When they think leaders are making arbitrary decisions that result in change, especially when they don't know why, they tend to push back and rise up against it. What would it look like to reframe the thinking about the technology we're using for the people in the room, while simultaneously creating a more compelling and transcendent experience at home? I'd challenge you to explore it.

In the next chapter we will explore the final form of Both/And worship, which I call Post Both/And worship. If the first two options haven't felt right for your church, perhaps you'll find what you're looking for in this one.

CHAPTER 5 POST BOTH/AND WORSHIP

"Don't worry, we'll fix it in post!"

-Unknown

It's a common filmmaking trope to hear directors utter the words, "We'll fix it in post" during the process of filming a movie or television show. While this lighthearted notion can be a funny quip for a behind-the-scenes interview, there are many aspects of film and television that can be fixed in post.

As explained on tvtropes.org, "Post-production, known as "post" for short, is the part of a film's production process that occurs after principal photography is complete. "Post" is where the film is edited into a coherent story, sound effects are added, and (most notably) visual effects are created."[1] Fixing it in post works in both film and television, but it also works for the process of capturing and delivering worship for churches who don't have the internet bandwidth, teams, or aptitude for Pre Both/And or Real Time Both/And worship. In some ways, this is the easiest of the Both/And models. It's even possible for a church with no internet in the building to have effective hybrid worship.

Here's how I define it:

WHAT IS POST BOTH/AND WORSHIP?

Post Both/And worship is worship that is recorded live with a future online audience in mind but offered only to the in-person audience in real

1. "Fix It in Post," TVTropes, accessed September 21, 2021, https://tvtropes.org/pmwiki/pmwiki.php/Main/FixItInPost.

time. The worship is captured, edited, and repurposed for an online audience on a delay. With Post Both/And worship, you have the freedom to largely go about worship as you would have pre-pandemic by recording everything that's taking place during the live experience with people in the room. You only have to make a few minor tweaks.

First, you still have to speak to your whole congregation. In this scenario, they're either participating with you in the room in real time, or they're watching on delay. There is no livestream option. Make sure you look at the camera from time to time. Leave room for them to reflect on what you're saying by talking to them directly. You can still engage with them in the chat when you first premiere the video, which means you can ask a reflection question, take prayer requests, and interact with participants during the premiere. Many of the lessons from Pre Both/And worship apply here.

There are of course upsides and downsides with this model too. Here are the upsides:

1) THIS MODEL REQUIRES THE LEAST AMOUNT OF EFFORT ON SUNDAY

With Post Both/And worship, you don't have to engage in a lot of preproduction. You can, but you can also just show up and do worship like you would have prior to March 2020. You don't have to worry about the internet connection and having someone monitoring it. You also don't have to worry (during the recording) about interacting with people in the chat; that'll come later.

2) THIS METHOD ALLOWS YOU TO KILL TWO BIRDS WITH ONE STONE

Everything you're preparing for Sunday morning for your live audience (part of your congregation) is also being captured for your on-delay audience (the other part of your congregation). You're not doubling up by recording everything and then doing it live like in Pre Both/And worship, and you're not having to try and split your attention in the same way that you have to in Real Time Both/And worship. You do need to be mindful of participation for those on-delay, but it's a little different in this model.

3) FEWER VOLUNTEERS ARE REQUIRED

While I've seen lone pastors or a small team of leaders be involved at every level, the other two models require more people. When prerecording, you have to be concerned with people in front of and behind the camera.

With real time, you must have people monitoring the feed, running cameras, and working the chat. With this model, you can reduce the volunteer load. You need to have your camera or cameras positioned well, and someone needs to hit record, but this is the easiest version for a one-person (or a limited person) show.

4) NO INTERNET REQUIRED

A large number of churches that have attended my Both/And training have been small, rural churches. Many of them do not have fast enough internet in their area to stream in real time. With this model, you are capturing what you do, and then you can upload it and share it with your congregation at a later time.

There are some downsides to this model too:

1) EDITING MAY BE REQUIRED

If your worship is an hour or more in-person, and you'd like to just do it as you typically have (at that length), you may need to edit your video before posting it to your platform(s). Just as recommended with Pre Both/And worship, cut the music down a bit. If you have long transitions, reduce those. You might even edit the sermon some. Remember, the sweet spot is between 25-35 minutes with a maximum of 40.

2) CONTENT MAY NOT FEEL AS FRESH

Post Both/And worship means that you'll be posting on delay. For some churches it is feasible that you'll have it posted the same day. For others, more time may be needed. If you are strictly on a Post Both/And model, some content will feel less fresh. For example, posting a Mother's Day, Father's Day, or Easter service the following week will create some challenges. Perhaps on those weeks you might opt for a prerecorded model.

3) YOU MAY FAVOR THE IN-PERSON CROWD

As good as our intentions are to serve all of the audiences that make up our congregations, when they are out of sight, they can easily become out of mind. And when they're not worshiping online in real time, it becomes even harder to remember those on delay.

It is imperative we develop good language for an on-delay audience. We've covered this before, but it's important to be careful about your temporal language. Try to be more generic, because everyone in this audience isn't watching it as you are doing it.

Post Both/And worship is probably the best model for smaller, less tech-savvy, less funded churches. It can have an enormous impact, and it means that every church can serve both people in the building and those online.

My absolute favorite church to talk about who is doing this is a small church in Ohio. Their name will tell you everything you need to know about them, and even yourself if you're doubting you can do this. The church's name is "Farmersville United Methodist Church." They are most decidedly not in the city. They are not a large church. They do not have an enormous budget. They do have a tech-savvy volunteer, but they do not have the most high-end equipment installed in their fairly traditional sanctuary.

Farmersville meets each Sunday in person at 9:00 AM. This is their only in-person gathering. As they begin worship, they record everything they're doing. The pastor and other leaders are careful to look at the cameras just as they do the people in the room from time to time. They do pretty much all of the things they used to before Covid.

During the week, they prerecord a few announcements and a few other elements as needed and have them ready to go in a video editing program. When the service ends at 9:45 or 9:50, they immediately pull the recording and get to editing. Basically, they take a couple of the songs, the sermon, and one or two other elements and add it to what was prerecorded. They then export it for upload. If I'm not mistaken, they drive it into the city where it can be uploaded using broadband internet. By 11:00 AM it is online for those who are not participating in the building. This means you can either come to in-person worship live at 9:00 AM or attend online at 11:00 AM. The people online are getting an experience curated for them as are the people who come in person to the building.

You might think, "Well, you don't understand, Jason. We're a small church." So is Farmersville. They've made it a part of their weekly routine to deliver this experience in a Both/And way because they value all of the audiences that make up their congregation.

Now, that may feel a little aggressive for you; it may seem way too difficult to make that happen on a weekly basis. If that's true for your church, you might just consider offsetting your online experience by one week - shoot it this Sunday, and air it the next. This is really only a problem for the first week, and for those high holy days mentioned earlier. You can always prerecord on those weeks. I know many churches who, before the pandemic, broadcast their services on local cable access stations. Usually those cannot be broadcast live, so they were always offset by a week. I've also known churches with multiple pastors, who rearrange series in order to preach the same sermon two weeks in a row at different campuses. The messages in the series may occur in a different order for each respective congregation but are just as effective as they might otherwise be.

Whatever the case may be at your church, whether you post it online that day or a week later, Post Both/And worship makes Both/And accessible for everyone. Keep in mind that a growing number of people are watching on-delay anyway. This isn't as scary as it may at first seem.

POST-EDITING YOUR REAL TIME BOTH/ AND SERVICE

Many churches who are opting for the real-time model might also consider doing a post-worship edit for their archived service online. After that service has ended, it becomes the archived experience for those watching on-delay. I've seen numerous churches choose to livestream their entire service which might go an hour or more. The audience least likely to participate in that sixty-minutes or more length is the one who watches on-delay.

Consider editing your service down after it's aired, to get it to that 25-40 sweet spot. Cut out those long transitions, the announcements, some of the songs, and other things that may not translate to an audience watching online on-demand. Sure, they can just skip past the parts that don't interest them, but wouldn't it be more engaging to craft an experience that's designed to be consolidated? And believe it or not, skipping is much more cumbersome than one might think.

Cutting it down can mean you retain the on-delay audience for the entire experience instead of parts of it. A church I recently visited told me that they experimented with the length of their post-edited service. They said when they made it 40 minutes, people would turn it off after about 30. When they edited it down to around 30, they'd only stay for about 25. When they edited it down to 25, most people watched the entire thing. Wouldn't it be better to get things to a place where they watch a little of everything rather than skipping pieces and parts?

Post-editing a real time archived service essentially gives you three distinct experiences of worship: one for people in the room in real time, one for those online worshiping in real time, and one for those on-delay. This option isn't necessary if you've applied the split the difference or staggered approaches covered in the last chapter. With those approaches you're doing the editing "on the fly" and your archived worship will be shorter and more palatable for an audience engaging later.

Post-Editing/Repackaging the Same Content

Similar to but different than applying a complete post-edit is the idea of repurposing your worship later in the week. You might consider giving people a small taste of your worship experience later in the week to tide them over or entice them into what's to come.

My friend M. Park Hunter, pastor of Onalaska United Methodist Church in Onalaska, Wisconsin, devised what he calls the "Wednesday Refresh." For each episode of the refresh, Park records a short new intro inviting participants in to either refresh their memories and experience of the previous week's service or to give them a refreshing message to make it through the rest of the week with an invite to the coming Sunday. The refresh is about one-third of the length of the typical Sunday service which is streamed live in real time.

The Perils of Changing Models

Every one of these three Both/And models has its strengths and weaknesses. In a season where the church is more malleable than ever before, it is possible to change from one model to the next and even back again, but it does come at some cost if you are not careful. After a period of time (maybe a year or more) of one experience, a change can feel extremely disconcerting to a congregation who felt connection in the previous model. This may feel like a decision that doesn't matter much, but I can tell you it can have a dramatic impact for the positive or negative. The intimacy that may be easier to capture with prerecorded worship may be lost when going real- time (where the camera isn't as close, and the pastor has to split attention). Going from real-time to prerecorded or Post Both/And could create less of a sense of interactivity and connection. Be extremely careful and ask what you have to gain and what you have to lose when moving between the various strategies. It can have an enormous positive or negative impact on your congregation.

As the pandemic we thought was coming close to an end found a resurgence in the late summer of 2020, I began hearing churches say that their online numbers dropped, but the people missing from the online audience didn't match the number of people who were present in the room again. Many were scratching their heads as to why the numbers didn't add up. I think to some extent this happened because churches stopped iterating, and things got way too templated. With the novelty of online worship in the rearview mirror, people were less excited about tuning in to the same old thing every week.

Another segment of churches changed models from totally online prerecorded worship to real-time livestreamed worship. The more people we had in the room, the less we thought about those on the other side of the camera. It was easy when they were all in the same place, on the other side of that lens.

At one church, the model changed from prerecorded Both/And worship to real-time when a pastoral change occurred. This church was doing some of the most engaging and intimate prerecorded worship I'd seen throughout the first year of the pandemic. In a matter of a couple of weeks, the decision was made to no longer prerecord sermons, music, and other elements and instead to put cameras back in the room and livestream the service. Shots went from closeup where musicians could be seen, expressions could be read on faces, and a feeling of connection could be felt at home, to shots from the back of the room where four of five musicians were all on camera at the same time. This meant head to toe wide shots where the facial features could no longer be distinguished. Body types and hairdos were the only real clue as to who was who. Gone were the closeups, direct looks into the camera from the pastor, and even the intentional language that was engrained in the prerecorded experience. There was a nearly 70% drop in live viewership in just a few weeks after the switch occurred. Some of that could be attributed to the return of some worshipers to the building, but the numbers didn't add up to what they'd been.

One person reached out and asked me, "What's happened to this service? I don't feel any connection to this now. It was so engaging before. What happened?" In giving the service a second look, I recognized the problem. In the switch from prerecording to real-time, there was very little consideration given to how an audience at home would experience the new model. Both/And language was easy with a prerecord. Everything in that model was about the online audience. The in-person experience was completely about the in-person experience as cameras were not used at that time. Now with trying to serve two audiences at the same time, very little attention was given to an audience who had only ever known being talked directly to for over a year. Where there was once deep connection, there was now a deep disconnect felt by many and the numbers reflected this change.

I do not fault this church for trying something new. After all, I'm a champion of iterating. It's hard shifting paradigms, and so much of what we tried in 2020/2021 was brand new. So how does one shift models and not lose the essence of what's been present in the previous model? Revisit the section on creating a Both/And Think Tank and commit to wrestling through that process. Assign advocates.

Assign an Online Advocate

Another way to ensure you do not lose your online worshiping audience in the shift from one model to another is to assign, empower, and listen to the feedback of an online advocate. This can be someone from your staff, a trusted friend, a family member, someone from another church, a consultant, or any number of other people who will worship online and advocate for that audience. I highly recommend this person not sit in your church's worship space as worshiping is happening in real time. There's too much they can see and hear and that can taint the experience of watching the team.

Here are some questions to ask as your online advocate worships from another room in the building:

1) What about this experience is working/not working that used to?

2) Does it feel like they're still talking to me?

3) Are they still using language that includes me in the experience?

4) Can I hear and see everyone (facial features are important)?

5) Do I feel like a valued member of the congregation?

6) Is the chat feature being used effectively in the new model?

7) Does there continue to be invitations for me to take next steps (connect card/action steps)?

These and more questions might be helpful for anyone switching models.

Let me also be clear in saying that I believe every model can work, and every church can switch from one to another effectively. It's not that prerecord is better than real-time, or even post-editing. It's that if we don't intentionally think about what we've done to the experience for people who were used to one model, we may fail to retain them when we switch.

An Honorable Mention Both/And Model

In some of my seminars, people have pushed back at the idea that worship would be truncated in any way. They lament the idea of cutting things down for an online audience, and they raise objections about how their regulars will feel about such edits being made to their worship experience. Some have said, "Our people want the entire experience from the opening note of the prelude to the closing note of the postlude." This is very likely true for some churches. I think every church must decide if their online worship experience is meant primarily for the people you already have, the people you want to reach, or both. There is no wrong answer. There is only naming it and intentionally trying to serve that audience.

I have always tended to want to create an experience of worship that speaks to those already in the fold with a strong emphasis on bridging language for those not already in it. As I see it, this was always Jesus' model. He spent his time outside the temple teaching with images and stories.

The idea of consolidating worship is largely rooted in a desire to make it more engaging for those who are not already a part of our worshiping communities. I wholeheartedly believe that whether you're a church member or a regular attendee, the online experience is harder to stay engaged with from home, but it's dramatically easier when you're already committed than when you're an outsider.

So, what do you do for those regulars who don't want to see a shortened service? Earlier I wrote that the NFL would never put a camera in the nosebleed seats and broadcast the game that way. I stated that no one would ever watch the players running around like little ants on the field. Well, I fibbed. There are those superfans who love their teams so much, they'd tune in even for that. They're so committed, they don't mind the far away camera. They know all of the players' names and numbers by heart. If you've got superfans in your church who would scoff at the idea that you'd only include a few songs in a prerecorded or post-edited service, or who would not want to participate in a staggered approach worship experience, there is one other option I'll concede here. You could call it "The Fly on The Wall" Both/And experience or "The Back Stage Pass" Both/And experience. The idea is that you'd have the less frills entire experience version of the service for those who want the whole thing. Maybe this is a Zoom version of your worship with a single camera, or if you have the resources to have multiple cameras and a team to run them, you could even do a live switch for those participating. The purpose of this option is to give your superfans access to every single moment of worship as if they were in the building with you.

I would not recommend this being advertised publicly to the masses. It's really not the best option for outsiders. It's a way to compromise and reach the already committed members of your community. Those who are just curious would be much more drawn in by the consolidated experience.

CONCLUSION
TO BE CONTINUED: THE "WHY" OF BOTH/AND

Can we stop doing this now?

-Recent Seminar Participant

In June of 2021, I was invited to do an in-person secret worshiper consultation and training on hybrid worship for a church in Green Lake, Wisconsin. Midway through my day-long training, a very well-intentioned gentleman approached me to ask a question he had appeared to be holding on to throughout the whole morning.

He said, "Jason, can we stop doing this now?" I said, "Stop doing what?" He responded, "Hybrid worship. Ninety percent of our people are back in the building now, and I just don't know if it's worth all the effort to continue this." I promptly responded with a bold, "No, my friend, you can't and shouldn't stop doing hybrid worship." I went into many of the whys which I'll share in this chapter.

The following morning, I sat in worship feverishly taking notes about my observations of the in-person worship experience. These would be shared an hour later over lunch during my verbal secret worshiper report. When the experience concluded, a woman full of curiosity at the end of the aisle leaned over to me and said, "Are you a blogger?" I said, "Excuse me?" She said, "Oh I noticed you were taking a lot of notes, I thought maybe you were a blogger." I said, "No, I'm a consultant, and I'm here to help your church with their online and in-person worship strategies." She lit up! She promptly responded by saying, "Please tell them they're doing such a great job. We're new to this area, and we only found this church because they had a Good Friday service online. It was the only one we could find. We were so impressed with the service, that we started watching the weekly worship online, and when they reopened the building a few weeks ago, we've been here every week since. We would have never known about this church if it wasn't for their online ministry."

During the lunch conversation I shared this story and the gentleman I mentioned earlier blurted out, "Okay, I'm convinced. We need to keep this going." I had to explain to the rest of the room what he was referring to. We all laughed together as I shared the story.

In the later months of 2021, I began hearing more and more leaders ask the same question the gentleman asked me during the training session, "Can we stop now?" I get it. We are weary. It's been exhausting for many. This has been the most challenging season of ministry most of us have ever experienced.

One of my dearest friends, who is a pastor and one of the most gifted leaders I know, said to me in a recent conversation that if a national shutdown of in-person gatherings occurs again, he may leave the ministry. This wasn't hyperbole. He was sincere. After nearly two years of doing ministry in a pandemic, he's not got a whole lot left.

Add to that that we are living in an extremely divided society, and pastors are having to play referee on issues of safety surrounding masks, distancing, vaccines – all of which have been politicized. It is a difficult time to lead, so wanting to throw in the towel on this latest thing many were forced into makes sense.

Let's also acknowledge that we didn't have a lot of time to strategize and had to wade into this thing step by step. We had a week or maybe two. Our resolve for truly hybrid worship wanes a little bit more with each face that we see before us in the building. Let me remind you again that we're living in a Great Commission moment, and "for such a time as this" we might just be able to find our second wind rather than throw in the towel.

I've recently begun leading a second set of webinars entitled "Both/And: To Be Continued." This training is meant to address the fatigue many are feeling, as well as address some of the other arguments people opposed to online worship are making. Because we didn't get to vision about this, for many churches this whole pandemic season has really been a "ready, fire, aim" approach. We started more with the "how" and the "what" and largely skipped over the "why" we should be doing this. It's never too late to explore your "why."

Know Your Why

In his famous viral TED Talk, "How Great Leaders Inspire Action" (and the book it's based on, Start with Why), Simon Sinek introduces the concept of what he calls "The Golden Circle."[1]

In his talk, Sinek diagrams three concentric circles with "why" being in the middle, "how" being in the next circle out, and "what" being in the outermost circle. Sinek explains that this Golden Circle demonstrates why some leaders (and their ideas) inspire and others fade away. He argues that every company and organization knows what they do, some know how they do it, and very few know why they do what they do. Beyond profit, they may not really know their purpose, belief, or why they exist. He suggests that we start with the easiest thing (the what), and we work our way toward the fuzziest thing (the why). Inspired leaders however, work the Golden Circle from the inside out. Sinek uses Apple computer as an example first with the outside-in model:

[What:] "We make great computers."

[How:] "They're beautifully designed, simple to use and user friendly."

[Why:] "Want to buy one?"

> That's how most marketing and sales are done, that's how we communicate interpersonally. We say what we do, we say how we're different or better, and we expect some sort of a behavior: a purchase, a vote, or something like that. Here's our new law firm: We have the best lawyers with the biggest clients, we always perform for our clients. Here's our new car: It gets great gas mileage, it has leather seats. Buy our car. But it's uninspiring.
>
> Here's how Apple actually communicates:

1. See the whole talk here: ted.com/talks/simon_sinek_how_great_leaders_inspire_action.

[WHY:] Everything we do, we believe in challenging the status quo. We believe in thinking differently.

[HOW:] The way we challenge the status quo is by making our products beautifully designed, simple to use and user friendly.

[WHAT:] We just happen to make great computers. Want to buy one?

> Totally different, right? You're ready to buy a computer from me. I just reversed the order of the information. What it proves to us is that people don't buy what you do; people buy why you do it.[2]

How does this apply to your Both/And worship? Unlike profit-driven companies, most churches know generally what their purpose in the world is but have maybe never considered what the "why" behind hybrid worship is. Many of us skipped right past that and started working outside-in on the Golden Circle.

In my training, another video puts an even finer point on it. In his series called "Break Time," Comedian Michael Jr. features a clip where he begins to talk to his audience during one of his comedy sets. He begins chatting with a man in the front of the room and asks him what he does for a living. The man tells Michael that he is a musical instructor at a military academy. Michael then asks him to sing something, suggesting "Amazing Grace." The man breaks into a wonderful rendition of the song, and the crowd is impressed. What happens next changes everything about his performance. Michael gives him some further instruction, asking if he can hear "the hood version" of "Amazing Grace."

The man begins to sing a version of the song with many more vocal flourishes, higher emotion, and greater impact. The crowd goes wild. Michael then frames the lesson like this:

"The first time I asked him to sing he knew what he was doing. The second time he knew why he was doing it. When you know your "why," your "what" becomes more impactful, because you're walking towards or in your purpose."[3]

---

2. Simon Sinek, "How Great Leaders Inspire Action," TED, accessed September 24, 2021, https://www.ted.com/talks/simon_sinek_how_great_leaders_inspire_action/transcript?language=en.

3. Michael Jr., "Know Your Why," YouTube, January 8, 2017, https://www.youtube.com/watch?v=1ytFB8TrkTo&t=6s.

You can see the entire clip here: https://www.youtube.com/watch?v=oVSTKpJBq-8

If you've never given thought to "why" you're doing hybrid worship beyond "because we had to; our buildings were shut down," now's the time to consider why Both/And must continue.

Thirteen Reasons to Underpin Your Why

1) Some of the people who have turned away have come back.

People leave the church all the time for all kinds of reasons. Maybe they didn't like a sermon you preached and they're mad at you. Maybe they liked the previous pastor more than you. Maybe the chairs were too uncomfortable, or the service was too boring. Whatever the case, Both/And worship has allowed them to sit in and maybe even reconnect with your church despite whatever feelings they once had. They've also been able to do it anonymously or without having to address their earlier departure.

I had one pastor tell me in a recent coaching call that he's seen three people who had left his church return since the building reopened. There was never any formal explanation, only the assumption that after a year or more of worshiping online, they warmed up to the idea of returning.

2) Those who felt shunned or were shunned have been able to participate without fear of condemnation.

People in church can be mean and insensitive sometimes. They can say very off-putting things to those with and without an established faith life.

I can remember at a young age attending a gathering at a church for a youth retreat called Chrysalis (the youth version of the Walk to Emmaus) and being told by an older person I should go home because I had a ball cap on. "This has no place in God's house," he said. I was probably 14 at the time and under that cap was the worst case of hat head you can imagine. I was not comfortable taking it off. My faith was well established at that time, but I might have bolted otherwise. I wore the cap anyway as I entered the building and prayed that God would not strike me down.

Being shunned for a ball cap is minor compared to what others have been through. Maybe someone's hair was too long, or they had too many tattoos. Others may not practice hygiene to the satisfaction of regulars, or maybe there's some other reason they'd not be welcomed.

In the spring of 2021, a pastor who attended my Both/And webinar shared a story that illustrated the importance of this second reason why we should continue Both/And worship. She told the story of one of her members who had celebrated her son's return to the church. This young man grew up in the church, was baptized, and went all the way through confirmation. When it became known that he was homosexual in high school, the church had a very negative reaction to this revelation. Whether he was actually shunned or felt shunned, he no longer felt welcome in church. He took a 10-year break, and during the pandemic, he began worshiping online with the church he'd grown up in.

Without fear of judgment, he could tune in and participate, rekindling his faith. Easter Sunday in 2021, he joined his mother in in-person worship for the first time in over a decade. Both/And worship opens opportunities for reconnection!

3) Shut-ins and those who are immobile and/or are suffering from illness have had the best experience of worship they've ever had since entering this category.

In some churches, those who are no longer able to make it to church because of advanced age, illness, or other challenges are out of sight and out of mind. Other churches have excellent visitation and care ministries in place, but worship has largely been an afterthought for these folks.

Churches who previously might send a CD, an audio recording, or a printed sermon for shut-ins to engage with, now have the ability to treat them with dignity and respect by including them in the chat, talking directly to them on camera, and by including Both/And language as they participate.

One pastor I consulted with took time at the beginning of worship to look directly at the camera and welcome those residents at two nursing homes the church partners with. He said, "Welcome this morning.

We wish you were here with us, and we're picturing all of your smiling faces here in the room." It was a beautiful moment.

There's another wonderful ministry opportunity involving shut-ins who are not shut in by choice, but by the criminal justice system. I've heard several stories this year of churches who have partnered with jails and correctional facilities to stream worship so that inmates might also participate in the life of the church. Some of these churches have even figured out how to partner with these institutions to allow families time to interact with their loved ones on camera as part of the service.

4) Vacationers, business travelers, and busy families can worship from anywhere anytime.

Sunday used to be pretty much off limits for things like soccer games, gymnastics tournaments, and the like. The "Blue Laws" of the past are long gone, and prior to our entering the streaming world, families had to choose church or those activities. Not anymore! With streaming worship, people can stream right from the field, or later that day when they get home from the game.

I've worshiped from a hotel room on many a business trip and family vacation. This relatively new phenomenon of streaming worship for some of us gives us a way to keep people connected to our faith communities while worshiping from the road.

5) Sunday morning (or whenever you offer worship) lives beyond Sunday.

For the early adopters, this one doesn't apply, but for all of those who first started streaming worship in 2020, it's almost hard to believe now that we put all of that effort and energy into one hour on Sunday (or whatever day you worshiped) without anyone but the people who came in person benefitting from it. Worship now lives on indefinitely, and people can be transformed by your worship service days, weeks, months, and even years later.

6) Visitors/guests can try you out in a much less vulnerable way.

Like going to an ice cream shop, online worship is the "taster spoon" for in-person worship. In other words, people can try you out before they commit to the more vulnerable in-person visit.

I've had numerous pastors and leaders tell me they've seen a huge uptick in guests since going online with worship. The funny thing is that those guests come in with some degree of experience for who's who and what's what in our worship experiences.

My friend Pastor Adam Diehl told me one Sunday morning he approached a couple that we didn't recognize to introduce himself. When he walked up and said, "Hi I'm Pastor Adam," they looked at him like, "Yeah, we know, we've been worshiping online with you for a long time." In just a matter of seconds, they all realized what had taken place in that moment and laughed about it.

This would be like going to see Jerry Seinfeld at a comedy show and having him come off stage to introduce himself to you. You'd probably think, "Yeah, we saw you on TV. That's why we're here."

7) Geography is no longer a limitation.

People can worship at your church from anywhere when you do Both/And worship. Worship used to happen at a certain time in a certain space. That's all changed. I've heard stories of families worshiping together from multiple states at an agreed upon time for worship, people reconnecting with a church they used to go to from other states, and people worshiping even from different countries. As mentioned earlier, The Chapel Online has 32 different countries represented.

I had one church in the Charlotte, North Carolina, area tell me that they had a family drive all the way up from Florida to join their church after being a dedicated online worshiper for months. They're not moving to Charlotte; they're staying in Florida, but they feel such a strong connection to this church, they wanted to step into membership.

8) Special needs families can experience a respite.

Having a special needs child is a challenge that many will never know or understand. Getting a special needs child to church can be very difficult, and participating in the "typical way" can be extremely challenging if not impossible. As the parent of a special needs child, I can tell you from personal experience there are times you feel judged by others when it comes to the behavior exhibited by a child who literally cannot control their actions.

There are some Sunday mornings - particularly when kids are younger - that it feels easier to just stay home. With Both/And worship, when those mornings come, families can worship without the feeling of judgment that sometimes accompanies the reality of having a special needs family member.

9) We can now dialogue with our congregations.

Worshipers both online and in-person can literally help shape the experience. I've already shared a few examples of what this looks like. With chat, Zoom, texts, and other means, you can deeply engage and interact with your congregation.

During a recent visit to Trinity UMC in Savannah, Georgia, I witnessed, pastor Ben Gosden demonstrate the power of dialogue in worship. With more than half of his congregation online, Ben devised a new way of offering "Joys and Concerns". For those unfamiliar with this language, it's more or less the sharing of things to celebrate and things to pray for (prayer requests).

In this historic Methodist church (the first in the state of Georgia) where the sanctuary is very traditional (thick stained glass windows, pipe organ) and where liturgical worship is practiced, Ben asked the congregation to do something very out of ordinary in such a space. He said, "This morning for those of you gathered here, I'm going to invite you to take out your phones. Mute them and navigate to our Facebook page. You can also scan the QR code on your bulletin to get there."

"At this time we're going to share our 'Joys and Concerns'." He went on to explain what that meant using language similar to the above. He then said, "We used to share these by shouting them out from our seats, but the people at home cannot shout loud enough for us to hear them, so we're all going to put them in the chat. That's for those of us here in the building and those online. Let's pray with our fingers this morning."

The chat began to fill up with joys and concerns from congregants participating from both in the room and online. Ben then pulled out his phone and began to share those responses. When he'd share a joy or concern, he'd make note of where it came from. For example, he said, "Sarah, I believe you're joining us from home this morning. You share a concern about a friend suffering from the effects of Covid. We hear your concern and lift it up now. Rob, you are with us in the building today and you're celebrating the birth of a new grandbaby. What a joy that is! We celebrate that with your family."

He continued on by reading every request. It was a beautiful moment that allowed a dialogue to play out regardless of where people were worshiping from.

10) Evangelism and sharing our faith have never been easier.

Many Christians are not comfortable sharing their faith with coworkers, family members, and friends. Asking them to church is an even greater fear. With social media, it's dramatically easier to share a link to a stream or a Facebook Group.

Encourage your church to make those invitations. Tell them where to link. Generate QR codes. Invite them to use hashtags.

11) Introverts and those with social anxiety can take a break from the stress of crowds.

Let me be clear in saying that I do not believe that introverts should bow out completely from in-person worship, but online can give them the occasional break when they're not feeling up to "people-ing".

As a recovering extrovert, I have a hard time wrapping my brain around the idea that being a part of a gathering and making small talk and connection is taxing for some. My wife however is a full-fledged introvert. I've seen how it can drain her. We're wired differently and I'm grateful for the perspective she gives me. When we go to a party, she'll sometimes say something like, "Can we go now? I've talked to three people." I'll say, "Not yet, there are three people I haven't talked to." When the pandemic first began and things shut down, she jokingly said to me, "I've been preparing for this my whole life." I know many people who feel this way.

For some, the greatest thing to come out of the pandemic is the absence of the introvert-dreaded ritual of "passing the peace" or greeting time. Our Both/And worship gives these folks a break when they just aren't up for socializing in person, but still want to worship.

12) Those with hearing and seeing difficulties can turn the volume up, sit closer at home, or even stream it from the room with closed captions turned on.

This one wasn't originally on my list, but in one conversation I was in with a cohort of pastors I coach, one pastor told me that this was one of the things she's heard over and over in her church made up of many elderly people. She said, "Some folks are at home watching with the volume cranked up, and they can see better with their device closer to their faces or their large screen TVs turned on."

13) It ain't over til' it's over.

I hope and pray that as you hold this book in your hands, the pandemic is over. In the late summer of 2021 (as I'm writing this book), it is inaccurate to say we are living in the "post-pandemic" world. The rise of the Delta Variant of Covid-19 is raging though communities large and small. Many schools have reinstituted online learning and mask mandates, and hospitals are once again overwhelmed with patients. Vaccine hesitancy is still a thing, and even the vaccinated are testing positive with breakthrough cases of the new variant.

We should not stop offering online worship and risk losing the skills we've developed. In the unlikely event we have to shut down the world again, we do not want to have to re-learn all of the things we spent 2020/2021 learning. Those muscles will atrophy in time. Besides, we've got 12 other great reasons to continue.

My good friend Paul Nixon and I were chatting about the importance of continuing these practices into the future. He offhandedly said to me, "Neither Macy's nor Methodists will survive without hybrid." This brutally honest truth applies well beyond Methodism, but he makes a great point.

We're living in a season of disruption and the church cannot ignore it. The movie industry has been completely disrupted by the pandemic with first-run movies dropping in theaters at the same time as at home. Services like "UberEats" and "Door Dash" have grown exponentially because of the pandemic. Grocery stores have developed "shop for you" services that allow customers to place orders online, then drive to the parking lot to pick it up without even entering the store. Schools - from grade school to grad school - have embraced online learning. The experience of worship has also experienced a disruption, a disruption that may mean some do not come back to the building.

Is Online Church Really Church?

Both/And worship and online-only worship have critics that question the validity of the online experience. Can it truly be church if they're not physically present in a brick-and-mortar space? How can we worship without physical embodiment? How do sacraments like communion and baptism work in this world?

Let me first state that this book is called Both/And worship, not either/or worship. I have never advocated that online worship be a total replacement for in-person worship. I've spent over twenty years writing about, speaking about, coaching, and consulting about in-person worship. It is my preferred form of worship most of the time. And yet, we should not dismiss or discount the power of transcendent experiences of worship online.

If you haven't figured it out yet, this isn't an academic book. It's written as a practical guide for those in the trenches. As I said from the opening chapter, I'll let others debate the finer theological points on such matters, and I truly hope you'll wrestle with these things. Still, the questions I've received about the validity of online worship have sent me on a few hour-long Facebook post rebuttals. Some of those things ended up in this chapter.

As Nona Jones points out in her book *From Social Media to Social Ministry*, for many church is no longer a building. She writes:

> Church is no longer a place. Google Insights reports that every month, more than thirty thousand people search Google using the phrase "church online." This means people are actively searching the internet to connect with a community of faith that doesn't require getting into a car to drive to an address.[4]

While the normative experience of church for many of us has been squarely experienced in the building, there are an increasing number of attendees who will make online their primary place of worship. This is hard for us to accept, but we have to wrestle with what it means for ministry in this present time. If someone first encounters church online and it is a meaningful encounter, they may never understand or see a need to come into the building.

The Disembodied Church

One of the pushbacks I've seen lauded by a few detractors of online worship is that it lacks physical embodiment. Embodied worship is the idea that our spirits engage physically in the experience of worship together in a tangible space. This experience includes the things we hear, see, touch, and

4. Nona Jones, *From Social Media to Social Ministry* (Grand Rapids, MI: Zondervan, 2020), 11.

in some cases taste and smell in the room. That physical experience might involve a handshake or a hug, but also includes the ability to hear voices lifted in unison. To pray together, recite liturgies together, sing together, and hear those vocalizations echoing off the stained-glass windows, decorative woodwork, and Gothic architecture (in some churches) is a beautiful thing.

As I have stated many times, not everything about in-person worship translates one-to-one from the physical world to the digital one.

During the first year of the pandemic, one of the things I missed most was going to the movie theater to see first-run films. I am a subscriber to HBO Max, a perk of being an AT&T Unlimited customer. This streaming service has an exclusive agreement with Warner Brothers to distribute films on the same day they are released in the theater. This means that I can watch Warner Brother's films from the comfort of my home at no additional cost, or I can pony up fifteen bucks and see them at our local theater while lounging in a heated motorized recliner.

A few months from the time I'm writing this book *The Matrix: Resurrections* will be released in theaters, while simultaneously being released on HBO Max. I was a huge fan of the original film, and while the series went downhill with the sequels, it's the kind of movie I'll usually go see on opening night in the theater. Despite the fact that I can basically see it for free, I will very likely buy tickets to watch it on opening night. Why? Well, there's nothing quite like seeing a film on the big screen, with an audience that is reacting right along with you in real time. It's a communal experience enhanced greatly by the smell and taste of freshly popped movie popcorn.

Watching at home on my large screen TV with microwave popcorn in hand while sitting on my couch is just not the same. Heck, I even have an HD projector and a 12' screen I could set up to watch it, but it's just so different than the embodied experience of seeing the film at the theater with other fans.

Embodiment is really hard to replicate in the online experience of worship. While we can take part in the holy eucharist from home, it is a different experience than being in the room and participating with a body of believers. Still, we ought not abandon this sacrament altogether because it looks different than what it has in the past.

Yale liturgist Professor Teresa Berger argues that "virtual" liturgy is still embodiment. She says, "God is omnipresent. God doesn't have any greater trouble encountering us in the digital social space than in a hospital room, a refugee camp, a middle-class parish in Connecticut, or in my own kitchen or garden."

She goes on to say:

> In fact, none of us can enter a digital social space without bodies. To be in a digital conversation with you right now, I need my eyes. I need my fingers to log in to Zoom, the space in which we've chosen to meet. There is no digital worship without bodies being present and involved.
>
> What is different, however, is that the bodily practices and proprieties are different from when we gather in a brick and-mortar sanctuary. For example, over Zoom I might have the luxury of participating without shoes or in sweatpants. That's a different way of being bodily present than in a brick-and-mortar sanctuary, but that doesn't mean we're not engaging in an embodied practice.
>
> Some bodily practices that are possible only over digital worship can be forms of enriching the liturgy. My local parish still has no in-person Masses; everything is online. So, during the livestream Masses, I've gotten used to dancing during the Gloria. If I did that in the brick-and-mortar space, someone would probably call a number I don't want to be called on me. But in the digital social space, there are freedoms of embodiment. That's not to say that digital worship is better than in-person worship. It's just not disembodied. It's differently embodied. I think of worship and praise of God as something that extends way beyond humans gathering in a sanctuary.[5]

The online experience is different but can still have deep meaning for its participants. It's not the same form of embodiment we experience in-person, but as Teresa points out there is another kind of embodiment happening.

If embodied worship is the only valid form of worship, what are the implications for shut-ins, those incarcerated, and those who are differently abled and cannot participate in the typical embodied ways?

---

5. "Virtual Liturgy Is Still Embodied, Says This Yale Liturgist," *U.S. Catholic* (interview), December 10, 2020, https://uscatholic.org/articles/202012/virtual-worship-is-still-embodied-liturgy-says-this-yale-liturgist/.

In a recent Facebook post, one pastor expressed concern that we are not thinking critically enough about the embodied nature of the church. He may be right, but I've been on a journey since the beginning of the pandemic to discover what the rites and rituals are for the online expression of worship.

Here was my response to his comment:

> I believe in Both/And, not either/or. One is not meant to replace the other in my view.
>
> Embodiment is a wonderful thing. I almost always prefer in-person over online. But I believe we limit the Holy Spirit's influence and power if we believe the Spirit can only move in one way.

In 2020, I was asked by a distant relative to help with an online funeral during the height of Covid. I set up a multi-camera shoot and streamed the memorial service live. Only a small number of family and friends could attend in person, but others joined from all over the country. At the end of the funeral, I sent out the link to be distributed and the responses I got back were enough to bring me to tears. People shared with me how important it was to them to 'be there' even if not in person. They got to 'participate' in Aurora's memorial. They were able to grieve and celebrate, and while it's not the same as embodiment, there was a deep connection felt by all.

Do I think all funerals should be conducted by streaming only? No, I do not. But to deny the power of the connection felt by a family united in the room and online is to deny the very real connections we can make to God and one another through this new wineskin of online worship.

Confusing Cultural Context and the Gospel

Over the course of 2020 and 2021, I've engaged in many conversations with critics who would rather not see online worship be continued. Some simply discount it as an invalid form of worship. I think it's important for anyone who believes in the power of Both/And worship to keep in mind that detractors of these new methodologies are likely launching their arguments from a place of fear and grief.

For many years in my trainings on creative worship, my former ministry partner Len Wilson and I used to say that people confused the cultural context in which they first encountered the Gospel with the Gospel itself.

Len would say it like this, "We confuse Jesus and the horse he rode in on in our lives." This was a much more Texan (where Len is from) way of making the same point.

A couple of decades ago, he and I were arguing with those resisting the installation and use of screens in worship. I remember people fighting about screens that might cover a cross or a pipe organ in worship spaces. Some acted as if they believed those things were inherently more holy than the fabric a screen is made of.

More than once, I had to remind people that that cross they'd covered up was not the actual cross Jesus died on - it was just a representation of it. And even though it was made of different material - wood instead of pixels and light - it was no more holy or valid than a picture of a cross projected on a screen. A hymnal is no more sacred than a screen full of lyrics. It may serve a different purpose, but it's not more holy. A printed Bible is no more holy than a Bible app on a device made of metal, glass, and microchips. The Living Word of God transcends the medium it appears on.

Some may want to lash out against and dismiss the present ministry realities we find ourselves in, fearing that the cultural context that we've found most meaningful in our lifetime may become less normative. What if those methods or some of the practices contained within them go by the wayside? We're ultimately not erasing the traditions and rituals of past iterations of worship with the move to online and hybrid; I believe we're reinvigorating them for a new time. We mustn't confuse the wine and the wineskin. We shouldn't worship the method, we should worship the God it points to.

My friend Nathan Webb, pastor of Checkpoint Church, offers a valuable perspective. His very unique church plant, which is presently based 100% online, uses the medium of online gaming to gather people who likely do not attend worship in person. In a recent Facebook post he expresses another point for consideration where fear is concerned:

> It might be helpful to remind ourselves that our current fear could be someone else's 'finally.' I've met more nones and dones in online communities than I could have imagined. I personally am a better minister online. Does that make my ministry illegitimate? Does that make those who are finally able to connect illegitimate? Just because we are grieving, afraid, or being forced to evolve doesn't immediately imply that this is the universal sentiment towards this change. Some of us, this

pastor included, are happy to finally be welcomed into the community church can offer.

Paul's Hybrid Church

Both/And should be continued because it's part of how our church was formed in the first place. Many of the scriptures we read today were formed in a Both/And model. My friend Amy Shreve pointed out to me Paul's work reflects a hybrid strategy. It had never occurred to me that Paul's combination of epistles and preaching throughout Acts represents both in-person ministry - where he preached in the same physical space with others - and letters that were written from afar (distanced).

We see in the scriptures that Paul was regularly longing to be with his brothers and sisters in person. He had an affectionate desire to be with them face-to-face even as he was crafting the letters that established the doctrine and how it was to play out in the early church. It was a Both/And model.

I find it ironic those who are dismissive of online worship do not bring the same critique to Paul's disembodied methods. A large percentage of our theology is based on letters penned by Paul using a hybrid approach. These things inform how we should live and carry out our faith even centuries later.

Discipleship Pathway and Relationship Building

I believe the future sustainability of online worship will be directly tied to our ability to build meaningful relationships with our Both/And worshipers. It should never be about acquiring views, subscribers, or influence with our social media channels. It should always be a push toward deeper connection and discipleship.

Building relationships may be easier in the building than online, but we must strive to do it via both avenues. Relationship building is where community begins. We can invite people into a discipleship process and deeper connection when we get to know them though intentional guest follow-up.

According to Carey Nieuwhof (quoting Tony Morgan's Unstuck Church Report), "only 21% of church leaders agreed that they have a 'well-defined digital ministry strategy to engage with people who are outside the church and outside the faith.' In other words, almost 80% don't."[6] This means that many of us have no real process to assimilate online guests into our communities and more importantly into meaningful relationships with Jesus Christ through our online worship.

Carey suggests that every church consider reallocating some of the money spent on in-person staffing to the staffing for online ministries. It's essential that we invite people into a deeper connection to Jesus through Bible study, prayer, and missional action. These things won't likely happen right away with newcomers online, but they'll never happen if we don't get serious about what the process looks like.

It's also worth regularly inviting online visitors and guests into those things within in a physical space too. Just don't get discouraged if they choose to participate exclusively online. And don't disparage them or the form by which they're engaging in your community. The connection some feel in the online space is very real.

Anne Bosarge, pastor of The Chapel Online, is excelling at this pathway to deeper relationships through online worship. I asked if she'd be willing to share their very well thought-out and executed discipleship pathway. She and her team have developed a very comprehensive and thorough process for building meaningful relationships with those who attend their online-only worship experience. Their pathway involves emails, invites to live prayer, worship opportunities, and even a personal visit from the pastor. Here's what it looks like:

Immediate Response upon Joining - Message from Anne

Hey there! I'm the Pastor at The Chapel Online! I'm so happy you joined our group! I hope you'll join in on our discussions about our faith and loving Jesus. We are a community from around the globe sharing the love we have for Jesus! Welcome to the group!

Step One - Welcome Message & Starbucks Gift Card

Hi! Thanks for joining The Chapel Online's Facebook group! We are a digital community of believers who are becoming more like Jesus for

6. Cary Nieuwhof, "3 Shocking Statistics That Show How Quickly, Radically (and Permanently?) Church Has Changed since 2020," *Cary Nieuwhof* (blog), March 11, 2021, https://careynieuwhof.com/3-statistics-that-show-how-quickly-radically-and-permanently-church-is-changing-in-2020/.

the sake of others. We have a weekly program called "The Difference" that premieres on Sundays at 9 AM EST in our Facebook Group and on our Facebook page. It is available on demand any time after that. The Difference is a time of teaching and worship that will encourage your soul and help you discover the One who makes all the difference!

In addition to The Difference, The Chapel Online offers a broad array of opportunities to grow in your faith through devotional posts, testimonies, teaching videos, prayer experiences, opportunities to engage online in community, and so much more. Dig in and let us know how we can help you grow to become more like Jesus for the sake of others.

Because you are new to The Chapel Online, we'd like to treat you to a cup of coffee! If you reply to this message with your e-mail, we'll send you a Starbucks gift card to thank you for being a part! If you don't have a Starbucks near you, we'd love to mail you a Chapel sticker. Just reply with your address and we will get one in the mail to you.

Thank you for being a part of this global community!

Step Two - Prayer Email

Hey ______,

Here at The Chapel Online we believe prayer is one of the most important aspects in our relationship with God that should be a daily, regular rhythm. Prayer can sometimes feel intimidating. Maybe you don't know what to say or feel like you're talking to the ceiling. Something that can help is just remembering that prayer is just an honest conversation between you and God – the same way you'd talk with a friend or a loved one. Try spending five minutes today just telling God how your day was and maybe asking Him to make you more aware of how He's moving.

We would love to be praying for you. If you have a prayer request you'd be willing to share with us, just reply to this email. We'd also like to invite you to join our WhatsApp Prayer Group. Simply follow this link to do so: https://chat.whatsapp.com/INW9daPRYqLEB3llarwpXb.

Have a wonderful week and don't forget to join us in The Chapel Online's Facebook Group this Sunday at 9 AM EST for this week's episode of The Difference.

Step Three - Discipleship Email

Hey ________,

How are things going? Are you growing closer to God? One of the best ways to grow closer to God is through reading His Word. If you're wondering where to start and how to study, we invite you to join us on Mondays at 1 PM EST in our Facebook group when one of our teachers will go live with a scripture study for the week. Join us live and ask some questions as we study or watch it back on demand when you have time. Let's grow together!

Have a wonderful week and don't forget to join us in The Chapel Online's Facebook Group this Sunday at 9 AM EST for this week's episode of The Difference!

Step Four - Personal Time with God

What do you do first thing in the morning? Do you check your phone? Make a pot of coffee? Wake your kids up to get ready for school? Fix your breakfast? What about spending time with God?

Time spent with God is what connects our heart to his heart. It's what centers our hearts, minds, and souls on what matters before we set out on our day. What does your routine of spending time with God look like?

We understand that it's easy to get stuck and be unsure of what to do when you're trying to implement a regular rhythm of personal time with God, so we want to help. We want to gift you with free access to RightNow Media (it's been nicknamed the Christian Netflix). RNM has over 10,000 resources that include devotional plans, kids' resources and videos, trainings, and more! To get your free access, all you have to do is text "RightNow THECHAPEL" to 414-11. It'll prompt you to create an account and then you're in! If you'd first like to learn more about RNM, you can visit their website at https://www.rightnowmedia.org.

If you have any questions, please don't hesitate to reply to this email. Have a wonderful week and don't forget to join us in The Chapel Online's Facebook Group this Sunday at 9 AM EST for this week's episode of The Difference.

Step Five - One on one with the pastor

(Send from Anne's email)

If you've continued to worship with The Chapel Online, you've been around long enough now to get the hang of things and figure out who we are and what we're about; however, we'd love to get to know you even better! I'd love to meet with you, get to know you, and answer any questions you may have. It's always great for me to hear the stories of people in our online community and discover what God is doing in their lives. If that's something you're up for, just reply to this email and let me know and we'll set it up!

Have a wonderful week and don't forget to join us in The Chapel Online's Facebook Group this Sunday at 9 AM EST for this week's episode of The Difference.

Step Six - Giving

Hey _____,

We appreciate you being a part of The Chapel Online Family. We are so thankful to be able to provide this online community of faith. The reason we are able to do this is through dedicated giving from the people in this community. There are a few different ways you can give.

The easiest I've found is Text to Give. All you do is text the dollar amount you'd like to give to the number "84321." If it's your first time giving it'll give you a few steps to complete. The next time all you'll have to do is text the dollar amount to 84321!

If you'd like to give on our website, just visit https://www.thechapelministries.com/give.

If you prefer to give via check, you can mail a check to The Chapel Ministries at 114 Harris Farm Road, Brunswick, GA, USA, 31520.

No matter which method you choose, we are thankful for your generous giving that allows us to continue to connect with people like you! Have a wonderful week and don't forget to join us in The Chapel Online's Facebook Group this Sunday at 9 AM EST for this week's episode of The Difference.[7]

7. "The Chapel Online Assimilation Process," The Chapel Online, July 22, 2021.

At the time of this writing, The Chapel Online has members worshiping regularly from 32 countries. The attendance is growing and steady, and people are finding real connection with each other and with God. While they are presently an online-only congregation, there are hopes and dreams of one day gathering in a physical space too.

Pastor Nathan Webb of Checkpoint Church – a church plant supported by the Western North Carolina Conference of the UMC - has begun working through the process of moving parishioners from newcomers to full-fledged church members. This church's parish is situated firmly in the world of online gaming. Nathan is reaching people who may never have been exposed to brick-and-mortar church and who may have no connection to God at all.

He says in building his assimilation process that he'd like to see it as levels of saying "yes" towards joining with the church. Here's his most current iteration of how that pathway looks:

> ***1. The easiest yes - Twitch***
>
> Twitch is the coffee shop equivalent of our parachute-drop church plant. It's totally open, totally welcoming, and also totally non-committal. We stream for the general public for around six hours a week and reach people from all over the world. Some folks talk in the chat box. Others don't ever say a word. If people are more curious or want to get more involved, we consistently invite people into Discord - our next level of yes.
>
> ***2. The first real yes - Discord***
>
> Discord is our church building, but more of a fellowship hall than a sanctuary. This is where people gather and build the foundation for community. It does require folks to provide some kind of consistent name. They are also joining our Discord server, rather than our Twitch streaming showing up on their feed. It's a next level that tells us that this person wants to learn more about this community and see if they feel like they belong. This does require some commitment, in the sense that they could leave at any time. Also, if they don't engage with conversation, then it doesn't work for them. It would be as useful to them as leaving the server. It requires action. After people feel comfortable on Discord, we consistently invite folks to engage with our next level of yes and first level of spiritual development - YouTube.

3. The Spirit enters the Room - YouTube

YouTube hosts all of our video content, which typically tends to lean more heavily into the spiritual side of the church. This is where we post our weekly sermon videos. It's where our nerd ministry podcast goes. We also have an immensely small YouTube following, so these are videos that wouldn't find many people - they have to reach out and find these videos mostly. Ideally, these videos elicit conversation either in the comment section or in a specified section of the Discord. After people begin to feel comfortable sharing spiritually, we enter our next level of yes - LVL2.

4. Stewardship of Self - LVL2

LVL2 is our most experimental step so far. This is our leadership program where we have an open form that anyone can fill out that allows them to sign up to be a leader in the community. It doesn't mean that they want to lead a Bible study necessarily, just that they are ready to move from the 'take' phase of content consumption to the 'give' phase of community engagement in our context. This has a series of perks as well as hopefully stewardship of time and presence (with great power comes great responsibility). These members provide us with their real names, real information, and real self so that we can fully welcome them into an incarnate form with the church body. It tells us that they are moving past being "one of the crowd" and are instead ready to start serving that crowd with their thoughts, time, and talents.[8]

These are the current four slopes of the funnel. They are still discerning financial stewardship and appointed leadership, but we are also – at the time of this writing - only a year into their plant.

While these are both examples of churches meeting primarily in the virtual space, churches who meet in a hybrid way should formulate and live out a plan to create community with the online space and in-person alike.

Measuring Success

One of the questions I constantly get from webinar participants and churches I coach is, "How are we supposed to take attendance?" I've seen a bunch of different formulas, and none of them really are anything more

8. Used with permission of Nathan Webb

than a slightly educated guess on how many are actually watching, in my opinion. When you saw this heading, your eyes might have widened in eager anticipation of a definitive answer. I'm sorry to say I cannot give that to you. What I would suggest is that instead of worrying about perfecting the formula, stop being so obsessed with attendance numbers. It's an old system, and "butts in seats" were never a great indicator for how effective your church is at reaching people and making disciples.

I can go to a gym every day, sit in the lobby, and watch people work out, but not improve my fitness one bit. I have to actually pick up the weights, engage in the programs, and do the work to make a real difference.

Perhaps instead of obsessing over analytic reports that most can barely decipher, we should start measuring how many people are participating in Bible study and online life groups. We might also look at giving. People give to things they believe in and are involved in. If you haven't implemented an online connect card, build one and track who uses it. If you're not doing guest follow-up or online attendance registration, those online people will always remain a mystery.

RESOURCES

BOTH/AND PRO TIPS

Over the last year, I've been sharing on social media some of the best quick tips for people doing Both/And worship. Some of these are touched on in other ways in the book, but this chapter is a collection of Both/And Pro tips for your consideration.

PREFLIGHT CHECK

We talked about the importance of properly preparing for Both/And worship. Don't leave the deployment in worship to chance. Develop a checklist of the common tasks that need to be done to hold a successful worship experience online and in person. I've worshiped with so many churches online where mics aren't on, feedback is in the sound system, graphics are wrong, and other preventable things are included in the online experience.

Block out where people will speak from and which mic they'll speak into. Have them sit in the most appropriate seat to get to their spot promptly. Make sure the mics have fresh batteries and are turned on before the leaders begin talking. Work through transitions from one element to another, making certain everyone has a shared understanding of the service. Test audio levels and play video clips all the way through. Check lighting, making sure there's adequate light for the camera. Check the focus and white balance of the camera if you have the ability to do so. You might even go as far as making an actual physical checklist sheet with boxes you mark as you go down the list. Because you likely have a number of different servants running the equipment from week to week, a checklist keeps everything consistent.

Remember, our guests judge us more harshly than our regulars, and while being perfect isn't necessary, we should eliminate as many distractions as possible.

SPEAK TO NOW

As hard as some of the things are that we've been going through during the pandemic, we need to speak to these moments and help people see them through the lens of God's kingdom. As much as we might want to avoid the pandemic, social distancing, and political and racial strife in these moments, we have to speak to what's going on in the world right now, rather than retreating from the issues.

For Easter 2020, I wrestled through this idea with the Western Pennsylvania Conference of the UMC who asked me to help them resource their churches since buildings would be closed on Easter morning. A team and I set about designing a package that would include graphics, videos, print pieces, sermons, and so on.

At first, we were tempted to just do the typical Easter thing, using images of butterflies, lilies, and bright colors. The more we thought about it, the more wrong it felt. We had to speak to the reality we were living in and remind people that the hope of the resurrection still brings hope to us today – even during a pandemic lockdown. After a lot of brainstorming, the resource set we came up with was titled "Hope Unlocked." The video made use of the image of closed doors to capture what was happening around us, but also to make a connection to the disciples locking themselves behind closed doors after Jesus' death. The video also drew parallels to the stone in front of the tomb, which felt like yet another locked door in their time. A voiceover provided the narrative, drawing these two ideas together. The video ended with a key turning in a lock and an invitation for the viewer to experience "Hope Unlocked." You can both see and download the resource set here:

https://midnightoilproductions.com/hope-unlocked-resource-set/

In designing this video, we were banking on the fact that people were regularly encountering closed doors (there were a lot of them back in March of 2020) and that those doors – redeemed by this theme - would become a reminder that there is hope in the resurrection of Jesus Christ. How are you speaking to "now" in your BOTH/AND worship?

Do also keep in mind that there is a balance to find between speaking to now and keeping things evergreen. Make sure you bring context for posterity's sake, so that the things you address today as you speak to now will also make sense tomorrow when someone discovers it.

EMBRACE HASHTAGS, QR CODES, AND LINKS

Equip your people to share your worship with friends, co-workers, strangers, and family alike. While this is a no-brainer for many, there are some still unfamiliar with hashtags and QR codes. I'm going to assume you know what a link is.

Hashtags are used to index topics, keywords, or ideas that are easily searchable on social media platforms. They use the # symbol in front of a word or phrase with no spaces in between. This allows you and others to track how people are engaging with your topic. The more unique you make your hashtag, the easier it is to track participation in it. So #bothand will bring up a lot of posts on social media not related to this topic because "both/and" is a phrase used for many things. But using a hashtag such as #bothandhybridbook is much more specific and is likely to generate results connected with a topic like this.

For fun, go right now to Facebook, Twitter, or Instagram and post something you've learned from the book and include the hashtag #bothandhybridbook. Next do a quick search of that hashtag and see if anyone else has had the same ah-ha moment you had.

QR codes (short for Quick Response) are a sort of digital barcode that allows you to embed links and other data. They can be read by a smartphone's camera app by simply opening the app and pointing the phone at the code. A link will then appear and take you to the embedded URL. There are tons of free QR code generators out there. One I've come to like quite a bit is www.qrcode-monkey.com. This generator is free and allows you to include color and logos and to implement some other cool customizations. Another QR code generator that is quite powerful and is absolutely free can be found at www.flowcode.com. It's a whole different take on the QR code idea with lots more customization possibilities than the standard codes do.

Do be mindful that some QR codes have expirations and others do not. There are also both static and dynamic QR codes. Static codes cannot be changed after they're generated. Dynamic codes use the same barcode but can be changed on the backend after they're published. Codes can be used for links to your worship stream, offering, digital version of your print piece, and pretty much anything you can think of. They're super easy to make and kind of fun to interact with. Consider making a quick tutorial to show people how to use them.

You can also offer good old-fashioned html links too. Just use the URL to your service, offering, or whatever. You might also consider using a link shortener like bit.ly or tinyurl.com to make those links less bulky and cumbersome. This allows you to create very short links without lots of characters after the slash.

CREATE A PLAN TO CONNECT

If you don't have a way for people to register attendance, sign in, or share their information with you online, there's no time like the present to get started. While people are sometimes hesitant to give out their information online – especially if they're new – collecting this info is one of the first steps in building meaningful relationships with potential parishioners. These services also allow you to track attendance online, and the more sophisticated systems allow you to track at a more granular level to stay in touch with regulars and newcomers alike.

There are numerous church attendance trackers out there and many interface with existing databases. Popular services like Breeze, Text in Church, and Tithe.ly are wonderful trackers, but if you don't have a budget for these, you might also consider using a service like flowcode.com which is entirely free (with a paid option if you'd like) to build your own tracker.

Invitations to connect should come on camera and in the chat, with links and QR codes easily accessible to online participants. Once you collect this info, be sure to let people know that you're glad they worshiped with you, and that you value their involvement in your faith community.

GET A SECOND OPINION

You are too close to your church, both in-person and online, to really be able to evaluate your own services of worship without bias. You don't mean to be, but you're partial. You can't really be totally objective, as much as you might try to be. Your opinion is good, but a second opinion (from an outsider) is even more valuable.

Over a decade ago I began conducting "secret worshiper" consultations for churches of all sizes, worship styles, and means. This is like secret shopping, but I'm not there to buy anything. The experience has opened my eyes to many things that churches can't often see for themselves but are happy to change once made aware of. Your guests (online and in-person) are never going to take the time to tell you where you missed the mark, but a trusted friend, colleague, family member, or consultant like myself will. While I'm happy to provide this service to any reader of this book and have done so for hundreds of congregations both online and in-person, you don't necessarily need to invest funds in having me or someone like me do it. Yes, I come with many years of experience, know what to look for, and what recommendations to make, but simply empowering someone outside your church to be brutally honest can provide you with a wealth of valuable information.

As hard as it is to hear about areas where we're falling short, knowing they exist is extremely helpful - if we're willing to do something about it, that is. More often than not, the recommendations that come out of these consultations are relatively easy fixes. It's a collection of small details that add up and take something to the next level.

WATCH YOUR LANGUAGE

Watch your language! Small language shifts go a long way in making everyone feel like they're a part of the experience. Avoid building-centric language and always give instruction for three groups:

- Those worshiping in-person
- Those worshiping in real time online
- Those worshiping on delay

Example:

"If you're with us in the building today you can [insert instructions for participatory act]. If you're with us online, you may [insert specific instruction], and if you're worshiping at a later time, you can [insert instructions]."

- The offering plate, basket, or box is in the room only. Tell them how to give online too.
- If someone wants to pray one-on-one, how can they do that both in the building and online and on delay?
- If you're welcoming newcomers, are you welcoming them both in-person and online? And if you have a first-time guest gift, how are you making it available to those not attending in-person?

GIVE THEM FACETIME

You've read this earlier, but it's worth mentioning again: looking directly into the camera during worship is essential for making those worshiping online feel like it's for them too. Whether you're a manuscript preacher, or if you preach from an outline, make some kind of indication in your notes to look at the camera at times throughout your sermon and throughout worship.

My friend Adam Diehl, pastor of New Hope Christian Center, inserts a large camera icon in several places throughout his notes. This gives him a visual cue when preaching to remember his at-home and on-delay audiences.

Eye contact is important, but don't look only to the camera, or your in-person crowd will feel like they're a studio audience.

LOWER THIRDS AND INTROS

If you have the ability to include an onscreen lower third graphic (the person's name and title), bring them up the very first time each person appears on camera. I've seen numerous worship experiences where the lower third comes up the third or fourth time a person speaks on camera. This means the lower third isn't shown until a sermon, even though the pastor has already spoken in worship. They may be a mystery face until that moment, so bring the third up right away. Even better, have the person introduce him or herself verbally in addition to bringing up the image on screen. A verbal introduction is more personable than a graphic. Introductions are just good hospitality in general. Don't make people guess who's who.

It's okay to bring the lower third up more than once. It is a common practice on documentary films and news magazine shows to see thirds come up numerous times to remind viewers of whom each of the participants is.

Finally, remember that everyone in the room and on screen is a mystery to outsiders until either a verbal introduction is spoken or a visual introduction is seen. They're all strangers until the introductions occur.

SHOW AND TELL

Because you're offering worship online now for people participating via screens, whether or not you have them in the building, show people what you're talking about in addition to telling them. If you're telling a story about that double rainbow in the mountains you witnessed on a trip, or that first car you owned as a kid, or whatever else you're referring to in story form, an image brings the story to life in new and exciting ways. It creates what I call "the lean in effect." It draws participants in even deeper than your words alone will. These don't have to be fancy/professionally-designed images. They can be snapshots from your phone, or images from Google.

According to an ongoing 2008 study, we are 65% visual learners, and learning increases by 400% when we use images to teach.[1] You can become 400% more effective by simply adding in a few key images throughout worship. These can illustrate announcements, scripture, sermon illustrations, and more. A picture is worth a thousand words. While you can paint a picture with your words, image (according to neuroscience) is better because it's the native language of our brain. Play to that!

TEST TUBE

Ever have trouble with getting flagged for copyright violations on YouTube? Want to know that before you're in a live broadcast? Set up a dummy account (not one connected to your church) on YouTube and premiere your video during off-hours when it's less likely to be seen. This will allow you to identify and fix any copyright issues that might otherwise shut you down.

I'd never thought of such a thing, but a seminar attendee of mine, Walter Vaughan of Marvin UMC in North Carolina, shared this tip about how they've fixed their copyright issues.

CLICKBAIT TITLES

How are you titling your weekly worship stream on Facebook and YouTube? Are you making it interesting and something worth clicking on? Or is it pretty boring?

Rather than titling your video in a utilitarian way, using the date, time, category of worship, and name of church (example: January 1, 2022, 9:00 AM, Contemporary Service, Acme Church), create a title that will be a draw for outsiders. My friend Pastor Chris Winterman first turned me on

1. "Studies Confirm the Power of Visuals to Engage Your Audience in eLearning," *SH!FT* (blog), https://www.shiftelearning.com/blog/bid/350326/studies-confirm-the-power-of-visuals-in-elearning

to this concept with his excellent reimagined online worship experience at his church TrinityOnline.Church.

The titles for your online experience of worship might even be a little different than what you use in the building. You might name the in-person service: "God Loves You!" The online might be: "Does God Hate Me?" Same sermon, different entry points.

HAVE A BACKUP

Every now and then, despite our best efforts, the technology fails us in the moment. Maybe the power went out or your computer crashed. Or perhaps, the platform was having issues, or something worse has gone down. When this happens, rather than forfeit worship, consider creating a backup that can be used in the event of an emergency. Record a few songs and a timeless sermon. Post it as an unpublished video on YouTube or even your website. In the unlikely event that things fail completely, you can post the URL to your backup service and usher people in that direction.

It may start out with words like, "If you're seeing this today, we've had a bit of a challenge, but we're not going to let that stop us from worshiping today!" You have time to really polish this one and make it great. Hopefully you never have to use it.

TELL THE WHOLE STORY

At the time of this writing, morale is very low in many churches. We're seeing a fraction of our people in the room and it's hard to process that. We can't figure out if this drop is driven by Covid fears, if its seasonal attendance dips, or if this is the new indefinite reality for what church looks like in person. It's disheartening. Our eyes are betraying us. When we rely only on what we see in the room, we miss a big part of the story. Yes, when we look out from the stage/chancel we see a lot more empty spots than we did before Covid. Or maybe we're on the opposite side, sitting in the seats/pews looking around and seeing less people than we used to see each week in worship.

Those numbers only tell part of the story. In most churches, the online numbers (real time and on delay) are still pretty high. We need to help our people in the room be more aware of those numbers. We need to give online participants a symbolic voice and find a way to help those in person visualize the folks we can't see.

I think it's time to bring back the old hymn/attendance/offering boards of the past. We should look at the analytics on all of our platforms (Facebook, YouTube, Church Online Platform, whatever you use) from the previous Sunday until the Saturday night before, and add them to the previous week's in-person attendance number.

Put the total sum of those two numbers up in front of people in the building so they can see there are people worshiping with your church that cannot be seen with their eyes. You can even use whatever multiplier formula you use to calculate online attendance if you'd like.

If your offering is steady (which it seems to be in most of the churches I'm coaching) tell that story too. People give when they feel connected and invested. Put those numbers up along with the online attendance numbers to tell the whole story.

It's not as bleak as we might think it to be. Empty rooms feel like failure. The physical gathering numbers are an incomplete picture of your impact. Take heart, its better than it looks.

MONDAY MORNING QUARTERBACK

Creating hybrid worship is a lot of work, and many involved in making it happen are so wrapped up in the development and deployment of it, they often never actually experience it. Have you ever taken the time to watch your worship service from start to finish as a team? If not, schedule a day to do that with your team now.

We cannot get better if we don't look back. In the same way football teams watch films to study plays and improve them, we should study our worship looking for ways to make it even more engaging and transformational. Schedule a time that is as long as your service with an additional thirty to forty-five minutes to reflect on what you observed. Do not fast forward, but watch from start to finish. With brutal honesty, talk about the parts of the service that kept you engaged. Which parts made you feel disconnected? Was there eye contact and Both/And language? Was it participatory? Basically, ask what can you learn, do more of, and less of? Keep iterating and innovating.

TIMESTAMP AND TRIM IT

As difficult as it might be for us to hear, many on-delay worshipers admit to not watching the whole service in its entirety. Many skip to the parts they are most interested in. Some skip right to the sermon. Rather than making it cumbersome to find those parts, forcing people to move the play indicator around on the timeline, you might consider timestamping your video to allow people to move through it with ease. YouTube makes this possible with a very simple process on the backend of each video.

Be aware that things like countdowns and looping announcements work much better live pre-service than they do on delay. These things work great for those gathered in the building, but most guests online are not going to show up 10 minutes early to watch that loop.

It is cumbersome to have to sift through 5 to 10 minutes of an announcement loop or countdown when watching on delay. My experience with Facebook's player is that you can skip ahead with relative ease, but going backwards results in the little spinning loading icon. Most of the time I have to refresh the page to go backwards, which can be cumbersome.

Either go live when you actually start the service, or go back and trim all of that extra stuff out for your archived version. Facebook's "Creator Studio" allows you to trim your video after your broadcast has been archived.

BREAK IT UP

Bite-size chunks may create more engagement for online viewers. In addition to posting your whole worship experience, consider breaking up the pieces and posting some of the segments as stand-alone videos. Both the sermon and music are great sharable moments when they're standing alone. There may be other elements like spoken word pieces, monologues, prayers, and so on that might deserve their own files too.

AVOID DISEMBODIED VOICES

One common mistake I see often in online worship is that of hearing disembodied voices of people that cannot be seen on camera. This problem is unique to the online experience. In the room you have the full field of view. You can turn your head and look around. Online you only have what the camera captures. Pastors, leaders, worship hosts, liturgists, and other speakers should be in place on camera before they start talking. If a graphic is on screen, it should promptly be brought down and switched to the camera that can show the person speaking at home.

Simply put, disembodied voices are weird. I've found in watching dozens of worship experiences that moments like these often cause me to look intently at the screen scanning back and forth in an attempt to find the person talking. Sometimes they are never seen.

Some churches include an insider ritual referred to as "Joys and Concerns." This is just fancy lingo for taking prayer requests and little things to be celebrated by the congregation. It's debatable whether these things should be included online for privacy reasons and HIPPA, but some have never considered that. If you're going to offer prayer requests, or Joys and Concerns, position the camera in a way that you can see the people offering them. Worship can feel very chaotic when there are random voices shouting out things that cannot be seen at home.

You might also consider eliminating these kinds of insider traditions from the stream all together and offering them as post-worship private Zoom meetings where privacy concerns are not as much of an issue. When you offer information publicly, it's out there forever.

MULTIPLE HYBRID WORSHIP

Hybrid worship can involve more than streaming to the web and people gathered in a physical space. During the pandemic, I've seen people extend their hybrid forms far beyond just those two methods. In my original training I identified three additional forms of physically distanced worship:

1) DRIVE-IN WORSHIP

Drive-In worship makes use of the parking lot as a worship space for those not comfortable entering the building. At the height of the pandemic, many churches realized what an asset they had in the form of a space normally reserved for parking our cars while we were worshiping inside the building. It allowed for safe, social distanced worship.

Some churches made use of FM transmitters to broadcast to car radios in real time. Others have used large sound systems, and I even saw a bullhorn or two used to preach the gospel on a Sunday morning. I've seen everything from flatbed trucks used as stages, to the construction of makeshift platforms composed of plywood and 2x4s. Others simply set up a canopy and stood under it at one end of the parking lot. With a strong enough data tower nearby, or if you have excellent Wi-Fi that reaches beyond the building, you can double up and stream from the parking lot online, while broadcasting audio to the FM transmitter.

Amy Vaughan, pastor of Marvin UMC in North Carolina makes use of a three-prong strategy that still uses the parking lot as a venue for worship. She streams online, has people worshiping in the room, and broadcasts through the FM transmitter for anyone who doesn't want to come into the building. It's a multi-streamed approach.

2) TELEPHONIC WORSHIP

Telephonic worship uses cell phone technology to broadcast to those who may not have fast internet or may struggle with technology. We must remember that those most susceptible to the effects of the virus tend to be older, which also happens to be the group that tends to struggle most with technology. Services like freeconferencecall.com or even Zoom (with a pro account) can give parishioners the opportunity to call in and listen to the worship in real time.

My friend, pastor George Reynolds (Linglestown Life Church, Pennsylvania), would do a multiple hybrid service by clipping a lapel mic to his collar which was plugged into his phone. While cameras captured his preaching for a streaming audience, people were also sitting in the worship space participating in real time. There were three points of connection: call in, stream online, or come in person to worship.

Another pastor friend named Lilanthi Ward told me she recorded a 10-minute version of her sermon to the church's answering machine for Sunday mornings. Parishioners could call in on one of three lines to listen to the sermon that had been prerecorded. This didn't even require a smart phone.

Remember that with the telephonic worship, you have to describe in greater detail what's happening in the room. Worship has to feel a little like a radio drama in some ways. In other words, you can't hold up the brand-new phone you got and say, "Look what I just got! Isn't it pretty? It's the latest model. I just love the shape. I'm going to carry this around with pride all week." For someone tuned in over the phone they're dying to know what you're talking about. None of those descriptors mentioned give it away. Instead say, "I got a brand-new phone. Isn't it pretty? They call this color space gray." Those verbal descriptions become very important to an audience listening in.

3) ANALOG WORSHIP

This is really old-school advice, but remembering those who struggle with technology means getting creative with other ways to engage them with worship. You may need to dig out an old computer with an optical drive and burn a DVD of your service. Print out your sermon and worship order and drop it in the mail. Make a mix tape if you have to. Just get it into their hands.

Whatever form it takes, analog worship is all about physical delivery. We must bring dignity and respect to our entire congregation and some of them need less sophisticated ways to worship with us in these times. Do not forget those who are not tech-savvy.

FORM A GEEK SQUAD

I've had more pastors than I can count tell me that their older people can't participate in online worship because they don't know how to use technology. That is such a huge challenge, and while I'd never expect that you'd take someone from "I know nothing" to "I'm a techno whiz," you can train people to use the technology.

One pastor told me in a cohort call that he was the pastor of a church in a retirement community. He said, "Most of my people do not know how to get on Zoom (their preferred platform)." He said, "I put the word out to my entire congregation asking who felt comfortable with technology enough to show someone the basics." He went on to say, "I had four people respond. I told them to meet me at the church for a night of strategizing." He said that the four of them started developing a standard multistep process to get people on Zoom, making up cards with pictures, icons, and so on. From there, they sent out a sign-up sheet to the whole congregation, asking who needed help getting online. Once the sign-up process was complete, the team disbursed, going into people's homes masked up, and distancing, with instruction cards in hand. They'd do a tutorial, show the card, and in many cases would load short cuts and automations to computers to make it as easy as possible.

This pastor told me that his congregation felt so cared for in this season. Not only did they feel valued by their pastor, they also learned how to use technology.

My own mother, who is 68, struggles with technology. In the early days of the pandemic, during the shutdown, she couldn't figure out how to get online to worship. My wife made it her weekly task to send a text with a URL in it, so all my mom had to do was click the link and worship would start. Eventually with repetition, she figured out how to do it on her own. I called this the "phone a friend approach."

We may be able to foster meaningful relationships between the (generally) young and tech-savvy and the (generally) older and less tech-savvy members of our churches.

TWEAK YOUR SITE

Your website is the front door to your church, and today it may be the only door people will come through. In a season where people are paying more attention to churches online than ever before, it's important that we give our front door an overhaul. Here are a few Both/And considerations:

1) TIMES AND LOCATION INFO

People want to know when to come to worship and where to come to worship. Worship times should be near the top and big enough to see with ease. It's the first felt need of a visitor. Since it's now possible for people worship with us geographically from anywhere, add your time zone to the worship times as well. You could very well have people from two or three time zones over wanting to tune in to your worship.

Location info should take on two forms now. Your physical address is one form, and the URL for your online worship the second. Make sure both of these are clickable. A visitor should be able to click on your address and have GPS coordinates launch on their device. They should be able to click on a link and find your streaming worship with ease.

2) WORSHIP DESCRIPTIONS

What kind of worship do you offer? Whether you offer one style or multiple styles of worship, it's extremely valuable to the outsider for you to set expectations for the worship you offer. How should they dress? Is it casual of formal? What kind of music do you offer? Is it traditional or non-traditional? All of these questions and more will help an outsider feel welcome when they come in-person or participate online.

3) STAFF OR TEAM SECTION

What we should ultimately be doing with online and in-person guests and visitors is building lasting relationships. The first step in any relationship starts with introductions. Many churches have teams rather than staffs, meaning they're not paid, but they are like staff. Include all of your leaders in this section. If you don't have a staff or team section on your site, get one going right away. Here's what you should include on it:

Photos – Every team member should have a photo and they should match style-wise. In other words, don't use a picture directory photo for one staff member, a glamour shot for another, a selfie for another, and so on. Take them all on the same day in the same location with the same lighting. Bonus if you can afford to bring in a professional photographer to capture them.

Vision Statement – Every team member should also write a paragraph or two about why they're passionate about the ministry they're doing at your church. Why do you love being the pastor of this church? Why do you love being the custodian? These paragraphs give people a sense of who you are even before they arrive in-person or attend online.

I'm much more excited about bringing my child to your church if your youth director says why he or she is passionate about raising up children in the way of Jesus than I am if there's just a name, title, and a photo posted.

Contact Info – Put a name, email address, or a phone number near your photo so that visitors can get in touch with any questions they might have. Invite them in the vision statement paragraphs to contact you.

Video Intro – During the pandemic, I've been encouraging church staffs to record short 30-45 second videos that contain some of the vision statement info, but also other moments that capture personality better than a photo and a paragraph will. Photos don't talk, and we've all read the wrong tone into the written word before. Videos give a sense of personality, and since we're meeting people differently now with social distancing and online worship, this is a good way to let people know who you are in a more organic way.

THE BOTH/AND AUDIT

In my Both/And webinars, I end the training by sharing a simple tool I've created to help churches audit their worship experiences in the planning stages. This can be used as an evaluation tool as well, but is best used as teams are dreaming about what they'll be deploying on a Sunday morning or whatever day they'll be worshiping. Regardless of which form you use (Pre, Real Time, or Post) these questions can help you insure a positive Both/And experience.

I'll also remind you to assign advocates to both in-person and online worship. Remember those who watch on delay when asking these questions

1. WHAT IS THE PURPOSE OF THIS ASPECT OF WORSHIP AND DOES IT TRANSLATE TOALL AUDIENCES?

Does what you're planning make sense for people in the room, at home worshiping in real time, and those worshiping on delay? Is it also friendly to guests? And is your language intentional for all four of these groups?

2. DOES THIS MOMENT BELONG IN ALL EXPERIENCES?

Not everything we do belongs in every expression and experience of worship. Some things work better in the room and other things work better online. Make the hard choices to do the right things for the right audiences.

3. IS THERE A PARTICIPATORY/EXPERIENTIAL WAY OF DOING THIS?

Without intentional planning of interactive moments, people participating online will always be watchers or viewers. We want them to be worshipers and participants. How can you make what you're doing experiential for in the room, online, and even on delay?

4. IS THIS TOO SHORT OR TOO LONG FOR EACH AUDIENCE?

Time feels different in the room than it does online. It's especially different on delay than it is in real time. What feels like it goes by very quickly can feel like it's stretching out forever when watched at a later time.

5. HOW DOES THIS TRANSLATE ON SCREEN AT HOME AND DO WE NEED AN ALTERNATE MOMENT?

We should be of two minds about moments that do not translate to those worshiping from home. We can do one thing for people in person and another for those gathered online. When we do things that are participatory, but impossible to engage in from home, alternate moments allow those moments their own form of engagement.

6. DOES THIS NEED ADDITIONAL CONTEXTUALIZATION FOR EITHER AUDIENCE?

The entire portal to the digital experience of worship is the screen and the camera feeding the image to it. An online viewer does not have peripheral vision or a full field of view that in-person worshipers enjoy. They can turn their heads to see what's happening. The online viewer is stuck with whatever is being broadcast. Sometimes additional contextualization is necessary to understand what is happening in the room. The same may be true for online.

During a recent visit to a church, the pastor noticed in the chat that several participants were commenting that the feed was freezing. Many in the room were not aware of this technical challenge, so he verbalized to those in the room and online that they were changing some things up while the problem was addressed. In this case, he was giving context to the room, of what was happening for those at home.

7. HOW WILL A FIRST-TIME VIEWER OR IN-PERSON GUEST RECEIVE THIS?

Our guests don't know us. They don't know our rituals, our practices, and do not yet love us. How will we communicate to them what they need to understand to be full participants both in the room and at home?

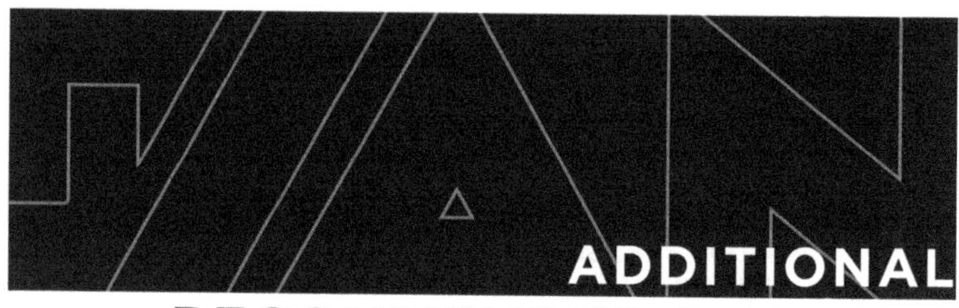

ADDITIONAL RECOMMENDED READING

As the pandemic unfolded, several authors released books to help leaders grapple with how to do ministry in this unusual ministry landscape. While I would have liked to have released this book in early 2021, I was so busy conducting trainings, I didn't have time to join these prophetic voices until now. I would have loved to have had the luxury of time to read all of these titles before writing Both/And, but it was only as I was completing the last chapter that I even had time to crack them open. In lieu of being able to incorporate some of the complementary ideas throughout this book, I thought I'd make a recommended reading list instead.

I've selected each of these titles for further reading because I believe they all have something of great value to offer. In some of them, you'll read about very similar strategies to what I've proposed, and in some cases, even similar language is used. In others, we differ in our approaches and recommendations, but I believe in bringing a well-rounded approach to your hybrid worship and ministry.

From Social Media to Social Ministry: A Guide to Digital Discipleship by Nona Jones

Nona Jones has been an incredible leader and an important voice in the world of hybrid ministry. She is the Director of "Faith-Based Partnerships" for Facebook as well as a local church pastor I first met Nona at a conference in 2018 when we were both keynote speakers. We've since spoken at dozens of conferences together. I was either her opening act or I followed her through much of 2020 and 2021.

In her book *From Social Media to Social Ministry: A Guide to Digital Discipleship*, Nona lays out a wonderful "Why, What, How" model for how to start a digital ministry. Understandably so, she makes the case for a

Facebook-centric approach.. I found it to be an insightful read with a good balance of theory and practice.

Fresh Expressions in a Digital Age: How the Church Can Prepare for a Post-Pandemic World by Michael Adam Beck and Rosario Picardo

Rosario "Roz" Picardo and Michael Beck are both personal friends, and Rosario and I have worked very closely together. Last year we co-authored *From Franchise to Local Dive: Maximizing Your Church by Discovering Your Contextual Flavor.*

Roz and Michael have written an extremely helpful resource that helps churches meet the challenges of what post-pandemic church looks like. The book is well-rounded and takes a holistic look at how to do everything from connecting better in worship on Sunday to how to do ministry from Monday through Saturday.

Being the Church in a Post-Pandemic World: Game Changers for the Post-Pandemic Church by Kay Kotan

Kay Kotan is a longtime friend and colleague with whom I've collaborated on many occasions. As of the writing of this book, she and I are leading trainings using the book I'm mentioning here and my Both/And material. The two dovetail very nicely.

In this extremely practical book, Kay walks readers through a series of helpful game-changing steps to rethink ministry in the post-pandemic church. Every chapter is chock-full of biblically rooted concepts and ideas. There are great reflection questions throughout, and the last part of the book offers a very handy "Re Playbook." This playbook is designed to help your church do the work of reimagining your ministry for a post-pandemic world.

The Post-Quarantine Church: Six Urgent Challenges + Opportunities That Will Determine the Future of Your Congregation by Thom S. Rainer

Thom is a well-respected thought leader and forward thinker who has written an excellent book on what to do in the aftermath of a quarantined church. His six challenges strike a balance between what happens in the room and online, helping readers rethink just about every aspect of ministry in a post-pandemic church.

Expanding the Expedition through Digital Ministry by Nicole Reilley

This book is one in a series called *The Greatest Expedition.* In it, Nicole Reilley beautifully walks readers through a journey of key considerations for how to do ministry in this present time.

What I love about Nicole's writing and her book is that she comes at online ministry not as a digital native, but as an immigrant. The questions she wrestles with and the solutions she's found come out of a lot of hard and intentional work. This will be both a challenging and comforting read for those who feel like they're lost in unfamiliar territory.

e-Vangelism: Creating and Implementing a Social Media Ministry for Outreach by Dr. Martin Luther Quick

I got to know Martin a few years back, but really reconnected in the summer of 2021 when the church he's an Associate Pastor at, Journey Church, hosted my Both/And training. Martin has built an incredible digital ministry, and his church has become one of my favorite churches to talk about when I'm teaching.

Martin takes a deep dive into what social media is, how to harness its power to serve the mission, and how it all comes together in the new mission field we're in. He also digs into some "how to" tips, giving readers multiple strategies for how to create a hybrid church model.

From Franchise to Local Dive: Multiplying Your Church by Discovering Your Contextual Flavor by Jason Moore and Rosario Picardo

March of 2020 was to be a celebratory month for my co-author Rosario Picardo and me. We were to officially launch our new book *From Franchise to Local Dive*. Then, of course, the pandemic changed all of that. We were set to do six events teaching on the material within it, but shelter-in-place orders brought about cancellations of those events. The book did launch but got a little lost in the shuffle of trying to rethink ministry. Thankfully, midway through 2021, the book started to find its audience, and we're doing a lot of trainings based on the book.

While the book isn't entirely focused on hybrid ministry, it is all about how to reformulate something old that needs to be revitalized, as well as how to create something new. Our aim is to help churches ask the right questions to form a recipe for ministry that is very contextual and which includes online. This book takes many of the lessons of Both/And to a deeper level.

Becoming Church: A Trail Guide for Starting Fresh Expressions by Luke Edwards

While Luke's book is not directly related to creating a hybrid church either, its content, process, and lessons all apply to what you've read in this book. I've had the great fortune to work with Luke over the course of 2021, and I'm happy to endorse him.

If you think about your Both/And ministry as a fresh expression of worship, Luke's book would be a great field guide to apply to the process of forming something new.